MOTION

OMOTAYO AJOKE ADEOLA

ISBN:

DEDICATION

Insert dedication text here. Insert dedication text here. Insert dedication text here. Insert dedication text here. Insert dedication text here. Insert dedication text here. Insert dedication text here. Insert dedication text here. Insert dedication text here. Insert dedication text here.

CONTENTS

ACKNOWLEDGMENTS

Insert acknowledgments text here. Insert acknowledgments text here. Insert acknowledgments text here. Insert acknowledgments text here. Insert acknowledgments text here. Insert acknowledgments text here. Insert acknowledgments text here. Insert acknowledgments text here. Insert acknowledgments text here. Insert acknowledgments text here.

1 CHAPTER NAME

How to read this book:

When it comes to the topic of emotions, most of us have grown up with many cultural, philosophical and theological perspectives, and we will be bringing all of those - including our personal understanding from our experiences - into the process of reading this book. I, also, went through this process in even being able to consider a different way to look at life. As with most significant changes we make, the decision to explore this topic at all, was the result of personal discomfort of my own. I have learnt that emotional pain has a way of forcing our attention to things that we would otherwise have dismissed or overlooked.

Because of my own process, my own skepticism, my tendency to search for intellectual discourse when exploring new idea, combined with my bias for the centrality of the love of God for me - and for all human beings, which I believe with my entire heart -, I tried my best to tackle the writing of this book from the perspective of intellectual rigour, emotional need and faith in God.

As such, MOTION is divided into three sections:

Section One sets up the premise of our relationship with God, which is His Love for us. It explores what love actually means: the depth of it, the sacrifice of it, the power of it and the emotions of it. God will pursue and woo and love on us until we are confident in His Love, and He does not expect us to make any sacrifices at all - not even "simple" obedience - until we have received His love.

Section Two explores Emotions in depth: what they are, how they function, and how intrinsic they are to our spiritual connection with God. Emotions are indicators that help us recognise how much of God's Love we have been able to receive, and with that knowledge, we can invite Holy Spirit to help us where we are struggling.

Section Three is a workbook to help us start to think through the ideas shared in the book. A few workbook elements run through the first two sections, but there is a separate third section that is solely dedicated to practicing and working through simple steps that can help us connect with our emotions by the help of Holy Spirit within us.

I wanted to make this book easy to read, relatable, and backed with in-depth bible study to support every point made, and so the different topics will have those elements:

- Introduction to the topic
- In-depth bible study
- And a personal story

If you're like me, you learn best from personal stories, because you want to see some evidence that the writer has lived out what they're talking about! It is after you've been able to connect with the stories that you can build up to the detailed bible study. If that's you, and you find yourself buried in the middle of a bible-study section, feel free to skip over to the personal story first, and then come back to the bible study.

And if you're a bible scholar who needs to see it in the bible first, because you are aware of how people can impose their personal stories on the bible and often end up misrepresenting the heart of God, you can skip the personal stories and dive straight into the bible study!

And if you're someone who reads books, nods and agrees with what's in there, but you don't know how to apply what you've read to your personal life, the workbook section is for you! You'll get to reflect, think through and practice what you've learnt, so that you can start walking in the reality of the freedom that this book will bring.

Plus, you can always reach out to me with any questions you might have. My email address is omotayo@firecatcherprojects.com. I look forward to hearing from you.

1. I'm not feeling it.

I'm going to be really honest. The problem with believing that God loves us is – well, let me speak for myself: the problem with fully leaning into and being able to receive what the Bible says about God's Love toward me – is that I have to do the work of loving myself on behalf of God. Unlike a physical human being who can call me on the phone, and give me a hug, and think of me and just send me a gift, or massage my shoulders when I'm tense, or any of those things; when it comes to Jesus, I have to do the work for both of us. Like, I have to do the work of showing Him Love through my prayers, bible study, quiet time, showing kindness to others, working hard and being diligent to fight the good fight of faith. I also have to be the one to remind myself, daily, how much He loves me, whether I feel it or not. I have to believe that, even if He didn't "call" me, He's thinking of me. I have to put myself in the position to hear Him, or He might not speak. Or, maybe He'll speak and I won't hear Him; I might confuse His voice with my imagination.

In real life, with a physical person, they can go above and beyond to show you in a tangible way, that they're there. And if they say, "Hello?" on the phone, you know it's them, and you can definitely hear them. Yeah, you'll still need to work on clarification during communication, and you'll still need to sort through the nuances of your culture and relational contexts, and there would still be misunderstandings every so often, but you can hear the person, and you can measure how much their actions reflect the promises they make to you. You can build a tangible track record of trust in your relationship.

With God, we 're required to constantly maintain of our faith, for fear that we would lose it: constantly affirming, declaring, repeating, memorising and reminding ourselves of the fact that we are loved, because it 's so easy for us to forget. We are taught from the pulpit that the reason we forget, the reason we need these constant reminders, is that we are human and our flesh is weak. But when we are loved by parents, or friends, or in romantic relationships, it is not because we are afraid that we declare our affections for each other. We share our feelings because we feel them, and because we want to reassure the one we loved of our affections for them. That is why they can trust that we are there for them: because we make the constant effort to show them how we feel, to remind them and to reassure them in difficult times. When it comes to God, however, the responsibility is entirely on us to remind ourselves of God 's love. And if we don 't receive His Love, we are taught that it is our fault; we are accused of not having the capacity to love ourselves on His behalf.

"Read the Word!"

"His Love is so clear!"

Okay, well, what He did that one time on the cross is clear, but that was ages ago. It's sort of like how the Founding Fathers of the country fought for our independence, years and years ago. But now, we 're independent. We 've **been** independent, and that has been my reality for my entire life. So, why do I have to actively work to generate consistent thanksgiving for the only reality I 've known?

Okay, maybe I haven 't "always" known it. I mean, almost every Christian 's journey begins with a conversion story, so we all have a memory of life before and life after our faith in Jesus. Maybe I should use a different illustration to describe what I mean.

I grew up in Nigeria and, even though the country had been an independent nation since 1960, by the time I was born in the mid-eighties, we were in a military dictatorship.

Even though I was a child, I experienced a little of what it felt like to live in fear, during the military coups. I remember my siblings and I being picked up from primary school because a coup had been announced in the middle of the school day; driving through streets where armed soldiers patrolled, looking out for anyone who didn't have the branch of a tree affixed to their windscreen as a show of solidarity. Journalists and activists were often killed for speaking up against the government, and that was just the order of the day.

So, when the military government peacefully handed over to democratic civilian rule in the year 1999, there was dancing and celebration in the streets of Nigeria. You know how the disciples of Jesus had been hoping for Jesus to take over from the corrupt Roman government and establish a physical Kingdom for the Jews?[1] Imagine what *that* triumphant entry would have looked and felt like: singing, chanting, weeping for joy, hopeful for the future! That's what the 29th of May, 1999, felt like.

But, not many years after, the relief that had followed the eradication of military oppression quickly transitioned into deep dissatisfaction as the new government tried – and failed – to find its feet. And for twenty-five years, there has been wave after wave of democratically elected suffering and poverty, as the political class continue to misappropriate public funds without conscience.

Before I continue, I know that it feels heretic to make this comparison, but here's the point I'm trying to make with this story. Sometimes, the pressure placed on Christians to love ourselves on behalf of God (*be thankful, or else!*) feels as oppressive as living under an uncaring government, but being reminded every day that, "At least it's

[1] Acts 1:6

better than military rule." Technically, yes. It is better to be able to claim the right to faith, to free will, to free movement, without oppression. But what use is freedom when the hospitals are understaffed and under-equipped? When the economy stifles business growth? When taxpayer funds are stolen and spent on lavish personal expenses, rather than to fix the roads and ensure uninterrupted electricity? Of what use is political freedom when all it comes with is the bondage of poverty?

In the same way, the relationship we are expected to have with God can often feel similarly oppressive: we are supposed to be quiet and stay grateful, even though we have questions, even though our needs are not met, even though our hearts are lonely. It's a bit like Stockholm syndrome: we don't have the choice to leave, and so we endure the oppression and call it love. But oppression is not love. Being forced into silent acceptance of pain, is not love. And **it was never God's intention for us to keep quiet and just be grateful we're alive**.

Love is responsive, caring, considerate and empathetic. It is gentle, kind and patient[2]. And, most importantly, when it comes to the expression of love - meaning: how we recognise it, how we feel it, and how we receive it - Love is active, proactive and tangible. That's how the Bible describes it:

"Herein is love, not that we loved God, but that he loved us, and sent his Son to be the propitiation for our sins." 1 John 4:10 (KJV)

This passage says to me that it is not **our** affections for God that are considered the ideal benchmark for defining or describing what love is. It is not our ability to keep quiet and endure, or our efforts to prove our worth through sacrificial prayer, offering or demonstrations of piety. Rather, it is God's love **for us** that led to His proactive act of Love (literally "catching a grenade" for us, in the words of Bruno Mars,

[2] 1 Corinthians 13

through His death on the cross) that defines love.

So, if – and since – His love is so extravagant, so passionate and so active, why is there such a massive disconnect in the way we are taught to experience His Love?

Why don 't we **feel** loved by God?

To a large degree, I believe it is because we are taught that we don't have to **feel** love to **be** loved.

One of the biggest arguments about romantic relationships is the idea that, "Love is not enough." The idea is that our emotional feelings are not enough to sustain the intentionality of effort and duty and commitment that goes into making romantic relationships last beyond the initial butterflies and attraction that brings two people together. That's a fair point, right?

Then there is the additional context of our upbringing and, while this varies widely, even within the same cultures, there is a general understanding that our parents are not expected to express affection toward us, as they raise us. Arguments about how parents are not supposed to be friends with their children, and how "gentle parenting" leads to lack of discipline abound, and some of our parents really took that to heart. Personally, the first time I consciously remember my dad trying to hug me was when I was around thirteen. Of course, he must have hugged me as a baby, and I was my dad's "handbag" until I was around five or six, so I must have received physical affection from him in those years. But I share this to explain that it was not common in my home. There were no "welcome home" hugs, no "sorry you're sick" back rubs, no casual touching when we passed by each other, no hand-holding, none of that. That is not an exaggeration. My parents never sat next to each other and rubbed shoulders, they never casually helped each other do those little things like button up a shirt, or brush dirt off - at least, never in front of us. My mum did have that habit of tapping you on the shoulder or thigh when she was watching something particularly tense or exciting on TV; I remember that. But I also remember feeling put off by it. It was like, "Uhm, we don't do that here." It is only now, as a grown up adult, that I realise how hard it must have been for her to have had to tuck herself in and fold her feelings away.

And so, when my dad tried to hug me, that day, I said to him, "Daddy, you can't raise us without hugging and then think it's going to change. It's too late."

I grew up in a time when aunties and uncles also didn't hug. It was a time when "elders" took pride in exacting strict greetings as a sign of being well brought-up, and the more informal greetings were considered disrespectful. This tradition even inspired a popular song by the saxophonist, Lagbaja, titled, "Mummy, hi." The musician sang about a young woman who was introduced to her boyfriend's mother. Instead of kneeling down as the Yoruba tribe dictates, the young lady simply said, "Mummy, hi!" This song was a humorous warning to all young women, on the proper mode of respect for elders.

Interestingly, by the time I was about sixteen or so, the culture had evolved. I woke up one day and found that aunties expected both my knees on the ground in respect, but they also expected me to give them warm hugs *and* even kiss their cheeks! Not only that, we started being judged not just on the respectfulness of our greeting (which was covered by the kneeling part), but on the warmth of our expressions! The young girl who didn't hug warmly was not as well-liked as the one who smiled cheerfully and air-kissed eagerly.

I remember being stunned at being forced into so much physical contact with people I barely knew. I used to be regarded as well-behaved, by virtue of being the quiet girl who would kneel down from a safe distance, then get up and leave, quietly. But all of a sudden, warmth and personality were added to the judging criteria, and I was ill-equipped. Thankfully, I eventually adapted, but just barely.

Beyond my personal gripe with traditional Yoruba greeting, however, there are several culturally accepted rhetorics when it comes to relations between parents and their children. From statements such as, "I brought you into this world, and I can take you out of it!" as a premise for physical punishment to using the children as pawns in fights between each other, and constantly comparing their children to other people's children (children who are raised by different parents and therefore, different values), being silenced and not allowed to express our personalities when they did not align with conventional expectations, there are many ways in which we were taught that we would not deserve to be loved unless we suppressed our nature, and conformed to an externally accepted image.

I am grateful to the internet for showing me that this experience was not limited to my corner of the world. If social media memes are anything to go by, it would appear that a lot of millennials and Gen-X'er's across the world can relate, to some degree.

But beyond the home, and the immediate social groups we grow up and do life in, the messaging from pulpits in our churches have also adapted this way of thinking into their interpretation of the Bible.

"If you give someone a gift and they don't thank you, will you give them again? Then why do you think God will continue to bless you if you don't give Him thanks? If you are not getting blessed, check your thanksgiving!" And the congregation shakes their heads in remorse and guilt. When I was younger, my mum taught me about giving thanks for everything and I ended up writing a list of things to remember to say Thank You for, including for our spoons and forks, for our beds and sheets, for the fan, for clothes, for breath and a home. And, of course we should be thankful, but the truth is that God gave us all those things even before we remembered to be thankful.

In that story in the bible - the one where only one person came back to thank Jesus after being healed[3] - Jesus healed them without requiring thanksgiving from them. All they had to do was ask. And even though nine of them didn't come back to say thanks, He did not take back their

[3] Luke 17:11-19

healing in retaliation for their lack of gratitude. He noticed it and, of course, He would have liked for all of them to come back with grateful hearts. But He did not punish them for it. The one who came back pleased Him, but His pleasure with one did not make Him turn back and lash out at the others.

We are also taught in church that hearing from God is a special gift that we have to work hard to earn, through fasting, prayer and acts of devotion. I want to be careful in how I address this, so I will use an analogy to explain my understanding.

In the relationship between parents and children, the parents are the ones who speak first. They are the ones who take the initiative to prompt the children to say their first words, to grow their vocabulary, and to learn to articulate themselves. As children grow older, they build on the foundation and support of their parents and teachers and increase in their ability to speak. As they advance in age, parents and teachers are able to assess whether or not their children are speaking enough, in comparison to the expectation of each stage of growth. And, finally, as time passes, their dependence on their parents evolves, and the children are able to initiate conversation without waiting for their parents to do so.

If we agree that God serves as our Father, in addition to being Creator, then our relationship follows the same pattern. We see it throughout the bible: God made Adam and spoke to him, first; teaching him and leading him. God spoke to Noah, first; giving him detailed instructions of what was expected of him. God spoke to Abraham, first, leading him on his journey of faith. God even spoke to Cain, immediately after he killed his brother. And even though He intended to punish him for the murder of his brother, He ended up putting a blessing of protection on him:

"… if anyone kills Cain, he will suffer vengeance seven times over. Then the Lord put a mark on Cain so that no one who found him would kill him." (Genesis 4:15 NIV)

God spoke first to king Nebuchadnezzar, to Pharaoh, and to all the idolators kings. God spoke first to Saul, who was persecuting the Christians. Jesus spoke first to Matthew and the disciples. He walked up to them and chose them, in their imperfection.

And, yes, there is growth and maturity in our relationship with God - and with that comes an increased ability to discern His voice and His instructions in different situations - but it is exactly the same way different children have different degrees of closeness with their parents. All the children have access, all the children have the physical ability to hear and to speak to their parents. But some children ask more questions, or spend more time, or feel more accepted than others. And the degree of closeness and the amount of time spent increases the frequency and ease of relationship between them.

You might be reading this and wondering, "So, why can't I hear? If it is so easy, Why haven't I heard?" You might be filled with frustration because you have tried in the past, or you might be worried that you can't tell the difference between God speaking, your imagination, and even the devil. I will come to that in the next chapter, but for this moment I want you to pause, take a deep breath, and just … imagine that you can hear. I mean it: literally, just close your eyes and paint a picture in your head of what it would look like if you could knock on God's door, walk into His office, sit across from Him and say, "Hi, Lord. Can I really just talk to You whenever I want?"

Now, I want you to write down whatever you felt in response.

Seriously! I'll even leave a few lines down below for you to physically write in this book, if you so choose. If you're listening to this or reading a digital book, feel free to open your notes app, scribble a few words or draw what you feel, if that feels more natural.

____

____

—

Another major teaching from the pulpit that makes us feel disqualified from easy access to God and to His love, is one that is repeated constantly and consistently:

"God does not care about your emotions."

"The problem is that we're praying emotional prayers!"

"God is not moved by your feelings!"

But, what about when the Bible said Jesus was moved with compassion by the weariness of the people?

"But when He saw the multitudes, He was moved with compassion for them, because they were weary and scattered, like sheep having no shepherd." Matthew 9:36 NKJV

Or when the Bible told us that Jesus knows how it feels to be human - not just in strength but also in weakness?

"For we do not have a High Priest who is unable to sympathise *and* understand our weaknesses *and* temptations, but One who has been tempted [knowing exactly how it feels to be human] in every respect as *we are, yet* without [committing any] sin." Hebrews 4:15 AMP

And in the Old Testament, what about when the Bible showed us that even when God gets angry, He turns around to give us comfort? Comfort is given in response to emotional feelings.

"And in that day thou shalt say, O Lord, I will praise thee: though thou wast angry with me, thine anger is turned away, and thou comfortedst me." Isaiah 12:1 KJV

What about How He promises that nothing can shake His compassion and love for us?

"Though the mountains be shaken and the hills be removed, yet my unfailing love for you will not be shaken nor my covenant of peace be removed," says the Lord, who has compassion on you." Isaiah 54:10 NIV

"I am convinced that neither death nor life, neither angels nor demons,[k] neither the present nor the future, nor any powers, [39] neither height nor depth, nor anything else in all creation, will be able to separate us from the love of God that is in Christ Jesus our Lord." Romans 8:38-39 NIV

"The Lord is gracious and compassionate, slow to anger and rich in love. The Lord is good to all; he has compassion on all he has made." Psalm 145:8-9 NIV

And before Jesus went to the cross, how about when He made sure that we heard Him confirming to God that He had shown us His love?

"and I have made Your name known to them, and will *continue to* make it known, so that the love with which You have loved Me may be in them [overwhelming their heart], and I [may be] in them." John 17:26 AMP

This leads to the teaching that often follows this one. It's the one that says, "Love is not a feeling."

Spoiler alert: I disagree with that statement. But before you shake your head in disapproval and throw this entire book away, let me tell you why.

2 CHAPTER NAME

Love: A Feeling, A Decision or An Action?

In the previous chapter, I pointed out that a lot of us feel disconnected from the idea that God loves us. We understand it, technically, and those of us who grew up with religion as part of our culture, have sat under years of teaching and instruction from pastors who emphasised the word, "Love" in their teaching, to the point where we can recite memory verses that talk about this love. However, when we experience moments of difficulty, we don't feel secure in the Love of God. What I mean is, when we struggle - either with loss, disappointment, unforgiveness, even temptation and wrong moral behaviour - we become unsure of whether or not His disappointment with our behaviour has created distance between us. Depending on the doctrines we have been raised to believe, some of us feel certain that wrong behaviour makes Him turn His back on us, and in response, we feel like we need to ask for forgiveness, and possibly follow that up with an act of penance - either through extensive prayer, self-denial (through fasting or other measures), atonement, offerings or other sacrificial acts.

This is not unreasonable, at all. In our interpersonal relationships, we have had fathers who get angry with us, and because of that anger we were not allowed to go on a holiday, or get a birthday gift, for instance. We have had romantic partners who would go completely silent and not communicate, because they are unhappy with something we did. We've had friends turn their backs on us and stop hanging out with us because we wronged them. We have had teachers penalise us for not doing our homework, or for failing at it. As such, we are familiar with the idea of having to contribute our own efforts in order to maintain relationships. And that makes sense.

There are two things I want to highlight at this point before we go further into the discussion.

1. Using the example of our biological parents, I want to highlight the fact that we are still their children even when they are upset with us. Our bad behaviour can not change our DNA; and if the offended parent needed a blood transfusion from the disrespectful child, they would still have the same blood type regardless of behaviour. **The first point I want us to note at this point is that family relationships can not be altered by behaviour**.
2. As a result of that point, the second thing I want to highlight is this: How do we know when our parents or friends are not happy with us? In fact, how do we know when anyone is upset or disappointed with us? **The second point I want us to note is that social cues (like approval, disapproval, pleasure and displeasure) are communicated through emotion.**

Okay, let's get back to the discussion.

As newborns, we do not have any concept of verbal language. The only means of communication we understand intuitively, is emotion. And emotion is universally understood. Tears signify sadness or discomfort. Laughter signifies happiness or pleasure. A child raises up its arms in a soundless request to be held, comforted or soothed. These emotional cues never change, even in adulthood.

Verbal language articulated through words, are built on the foundation of these emotional cues. When children are learning words, parents use gestures that indicate emotion, and then repeat sounds over and over to connect the gesture to the sounded word. For instance, a child learns that the word, "No!" is associated with denial of a request because a parent frowns and shakes their head while repeating it. The frown expresses the emotion of displeasure, and over time, the word, "No" is associated with it.

Even as adults, when communicating with strangers, we might run our bellies to signify hunger, or smile and nod to signify approval.

In summary, emotions are the language of all our non-verbal communication. We are born with the innate, intuitive ability to pick up on other people's emotions. This is what forms the basis of what we call our Body Language. Our bodies "speak" through our mannerisms and facial expressions, communicating things that our words are not able to convey. And our words help us say things that our bodies and emotions alone are not able to convey. They work together.

Consider the last time you had a disagreement with a close friend or parent. You probably felt frustrated because your words were misunderstood. Maybe you felt regret because you had hurt them, unintentionally. Maybe you miss them because you haven't spoken for a while, and now, you're no longer sure if you can just walk up to them to have a conversation. All those emotions are real, and they are important. It is because you miss them that you might go out of your way to try to figure out a way to reconcile.

In the same way, if you have been disappointed by someone you trusted, perhaps in a romantic relationship, you might feel confusion when their actions directly contradict the promises they made. Hurt and anger might follow, and if you are not able to come to an agreement, you might experience deep sadness and even grief for the loss of that connection. Emotions help us understand what we feel.

When we watch movies, read books or consume other forms of media and art, our emotions are stirred up: you feel connected to the character because of their portrayal of sadness or love. You feel like you can trust that reporter because you feel like they are honest in their communication.

Additionally, emotions are not one-directional: we can also choose to stir them up, to calm them down, or to direct them in whatever way suits the situation or the purpose. You play certain songs because they put you in a good mood to study, to exercise, or to dance. You move yourself from a state of anxiety into a state of calmness when you have a job interview or important presentation. You play soothing sounds to put you in a peaceful state when you want to sleep.

Or, you square your shoulders and speak in an authoritative tone when you want to come across as a serious person. You might also relax your shoulders, smile more and use your body language to convey interest when you find someone attractive. You take on a pleading tone when you're asking a favour, because you want to convince the other person to help you.

So far, I've been unpacking the fact that many of us don't feel God's Love. And, in response to this disconnected feeling we have, we are taught by preachers that it doesn't matter how we feel, because God supposedly does not care about our feelings: as long as the Bible tells us for a fact that He **does** love us, it doesn't matter whether or not we feel it in our emotions. We need to just repeat it to ourselves over and over, accept it and shove our silly feelings away, because they can not be trusted. After all, if our emotions tell us one thing, but God says something different, then our emotions must be lying to us. And we all know that the devil is the father of lies, therefore our lying feelings must have come from the devil, and therefore we must actively kill that lie before it kills, steals and destroys us.

Whew.

Okay, but hear me out: **our emotions are never lying to us.**

Let me explain.

It's like, a mirror. You might look in the mirror and hate the way you look. That is how you feel. Based on how you feel, you might choose to wear certain kinds of clothes - to hide your flaws, or to enhance your features. Or, you might ask a friend what they think, to try to boost your self-esteem. You might even decide to start saving up for plastic surgery. Or just realise you've been slacking on your exercise routine, and choose to take a long brisk walk.

But the mirror did not tell you what to do: the mirror simply reflected what was there.

In the same way, emotions are not instructions; they are signals. Some signals are more urgent than others, and some can be so quiet that we don't notice they were there for a really long time. Let's use the analogy of a car: there are loud signals: like the loud honk of a car horn when someone just walked into the road without looking. Or the beep that lets you know a door hasn't been closed properly. Then there's the light from the fuel gauge that comes on just under the quarter-tank level. Depending on where you are, you might be able to drive home without needing to top-up. Some feelings urge you to take immediate action, and others are just there to let you know you need to pay attention to something.

Before I connect this with our feelings about God's Love, I want us to think about our relationship with romantic partners. (If you currently don't have one, you're not alone - let's just use our imagination, or maybe think back to a relatively healthy one from the past.)

When you meet someone and there's mutual attraction, that feeling of interest is stirred up within us, and we make the decision to reach out, talk or send a DM. As you get to know each other, you gather information about each other, and this becomes the basis to decide whether or not you want to go into a committed relationship. Throughout this process, the initial attraction grows into affection, and you share these feelings with each other. Some people prefer frequent words of affirmation, some people prefer gifts, some people don't recognise any feelings unless they spend a lot of time with each other, some like to hold hands, hug and cuddle a lot, and some people do things for each other: "I'll pick you up!" "Let me do it for you." etc. That covers the commonly used Five Love Languages model, even though there are many other expressions of Love. A running joke on the Nigerian end of the internet states that our parents' love language is, "Have you eaten?" or, "I made [insert favourite food], it's in the kitchen."

One of the recurring problems in these relationships is that, after mutual commitment has been established, the expressions of love slow down or stop, altogether. It becomes, "You don't call me, anymore." "You don't do the things you used to do." "We don't spend any time together." And, depending on whether or not you broke up with the person you're thinking about for this illustration, that relationship eventually ended because the person could not muster enough interest to continue to invest effort into doing the things that expressed their feelings.

On the other hand, if you're thinking about a current relationship that is still going strong, then you would find that you needed to put in effort into showing love in a way that the other person could receive, and that's what has kept the relationship going strong.

The reality is that Love always begins as an emotion; a feeling. However, as we discussed with the Mirror analogy, feelings are reflections. So we can feel things strongly, but our feelings are not instructions. In order to communicate feelings, we must take a decision and move into action.

Mind, Will, Emotion:

Our emotions are not at war with our thoughts or our will. All three elements of our "soul" - the inner man - work *together,* within us.

The emotion is often the first part of us to be stirred up: we feel something inside us. When we are younger or less mature, it is difficult for us to manage our emotions - just look at babies who cry immediately they feel discomfort of any kind, and little children who throw tantrums when they don't get what they want.

As we grow up and become more mature, our thought life gets developed. We understand how to take in information, and how to use that information to consider, analyse, discuss, assess situations. Formal education opens us up to theories and philosophies from far and wide, while informal education exposes us to information through experience, word of mouth, practice, observation, etc.

As young children, we feel emotions and seem to jump straight to action, skipping the "thought" realm. As we mature, our thought realm develops and our minds are better equipped with information. This information helps us create a bridge between our emotions and the actions we eventually take: our thoughts are able to process the raw information reflected to us by the "mirror" of our feelings, so we can make informed choices.

Our will is present the entire time: we are always choosing what to do; whether we are leading with emotions alone, or whether we are choosing to involve our thoughts in the process of the decision-making.

Our emotions are also always present. We are physically unable to detach ourselves from our emotion. However, we can suppress them, ignore them, subdue them or manipulate them.

SOUL/ "Inner Man"

ELEMENT	FUNCTION	LOCATION
Mind	Thinking,Analysis, Questioning, Reasoning.	**Brain.**
Emotion	Feelings, Affections, Desires.	**Heart.**

Will	Decision-making, Action.	Action (carried out through the **Body**.)

In healthy situations and relationships, our feelings are welcomed, received, and reciprocated through actions. In unhealthy ones, our feelings are not welcome: they are dismissed, shut down, ignored, overlooked or manipulated.

So when we don't feel like God loves us, we are not saying that God does not love us. We are saying that we do not have an emotional witness within us, that confirms the fact of God's love in a way that makes us feel reassured, secure and confident that our relationship with Him is intact. Like our physical relationships where we need reassurance, affirmation, acts of service, physical touch, quality time or gifts, we also need reassurance of God's love.

God absolutely cares about our feelings. He understands our need for assurance. He does not get offended because we feel the need to check again, if He's still with us, if He's still pleased with us, if we've done something to upset Him. He is not upset when we ask for gifts, or signs, as evidence that He is still committed to us.

He does not get tired of us. He does not get irritated with us. He loves us - spiritually, emotionally, logically, and even physically.

How do you feel? Do you believe this? If you're listening to this or reading a digital book, feel free to open your notes app, scribble a few words or draw what you feel, if that feels more natural.

____

____

3 CHAPTER NAME

3. God's Love Language

"For I am persuaded, that neither death, nor life, nor angels, nor principalities, nor powers, nor things present, nor things to come, Nor height, nor depth, nor any other creature, shall be able to separate us from the love of God, which is in Christ Jesus our Lord."

—Romans 8:38-39 KJV

So if - and since - He loves us so much, how come we don't always feel it? And, on that note, how can we feel it - is it even possible? After all, God is invisible. The Bible says He lives in our hearts so that rules out warm hugs. At the same time, we live inside Him (somehow?) We believe these spiritual truths, but we are also burdened by the fact that we don't understand how to reconcile them with our physical lives.

And, sometimes, if you're like me, you might wonder why you were even created. It feels like a heavy responsibility that we were entrusted with, are expected to be grateful for, however we're completely unprepared to handle it. It's happens with some parents: they tell you all the ways you should be "more" something - more responsible, more respectful, more resourceful, more financially successful, etc. But depending on how you grew up, you might have felt like you were constantly failing at it. It's like, if I was such a failure, why did you have me? I didn't ask to be here!

God is aware of this dichotomy.

He knows we feel uncertain about what we can say, what we can ask for, what we can even ask Him, whether out of curiosity or out of pain or confusion or just general interest.

The Holy Books of the Old Testament depict God in ways that make Him out to be unapproachable, angry, cantankerous, impulsive, harsh and unfair. And in contrast, some pastors and teachers paint Him as a soft, fluffy God who lives in a cotton-candy throne, smiling at us constantly. None of those approaches encapsulate Him correctly or completely - and He knows that.

"For my thoughts are not your thoughts, neither are your ways my ways, saith the LORD. For as the heavens are higher than the earth, so are my ways higher than your ways, and my thoughts than your thoughts." (Isaiah 55:8-9 KJV)

Despite this, however, He does give us insight into His original intention behind creating us, the kind of relationship He longs to have with us, the kinds of interaction He invites us to share and experience with Him, and how He expresses His Love to us.

More importantly, before He put any pressure on us to do anything at all - to repent, to do good, to pray, to be spiritual, to forgive, to live out some great purpose - the first thing He did was give us His Love.

"In this was manifested the love of God toward us, because that God sent his only begotten Son into the world, that we might live through him." 1 John 4:9 (KJV)

Love was God's purpose. It motivated His action toward us. It is because of Love that there is a Christian faith - if Jesus did not come as evidence of God's Love, there would be no "believing" because there would be no one to believe in.

Love gives us purpose. It grounds us, it holds us up when we feel discouraged, it gives us a reason to persevere, and it makes all the ups and downs of the journey worth it. And the purpose of God's Love toward us, is for us "to be conformed to the image of his Son."[4] Basically, He wants us to be like Him.

And that is what He has always wanted, from the Beginning:

"And God said, Let us make man in our image, after our likeness: and let them have dominion…" Genesis 1:26 KJV

"And as we have borne the image of the man of dust, we shall also bear the image of the heavenly Man." 1 Corinthians 15:49 NKJV

"Herein is our love made perfect, […] as He is, so are we in this world." 1 John 4:17 KJV

But you already know this. Forgive me, I don't mean to go over old information just for the sake of it; I am only trying to invite you into a more emotional perspective of God's love. Like, imagine that truly God feels your feelings. He knows when you're just holding on, trying to encourage yourself - but you still feel disconnected. He knows when you're wondering what the point of everything is. And He knows that, sometimes, this idea of being made in His image and likeness just sounds like an unrealistic and, quite frankly, an unfair target to hit, because we are human beings! How can we ever know or do what it takes to be "as Christ is" on this side of eternity? This fallen world with

[4] Romans 8:29 KJV

all its troubles, sickness, disease, poverty, strife, injustice and corruption? Sometimes it feels like He set us up for failure. And even though we know, intellectually, and from reading the promises in the Bible, that that's not true (because God so loves us), the disconnect remains.

So let's "connect". Let's find out the ways in which this great, Loving God, intends to comfort us, reassure us, convince us, and communicate His Love to us.

"You have recorded [recounted] my troubles [wanderings]. You have kept a list of my tears [put my tears in your bottle]. Aren 't they in your records?"

— Psalm 56:8 EXB

"He has sent Me to heal the brokenhearted…"

— Isaiah 61:1 NKJV

"And God shall wipe away all tears from their eyes; and there shall be no more death, neither sorrow, nor crying, neither shall there be any more pain: for the former things are passed away."

— Revelation 21:4 KJV

God, The Initiator:

In our relationship with God, He makes the first move. From the Beginning, He was the one who set the scene, created the garden and invited us to join Him.

"In the beginning God created the heaven and the earth."

— Genesis 1:1 KJV

This continues throughout the Bible: It was God who called Abraham and invited him to come on the faith journey. It was not

Abraham who woke up one day and decided to pursue a relationship with God.

"Now the LORD had said unto Abram, Get thee out of thy country, and from thy kindred, and from thy father's house, unto a land that I will shew thee:"

— Genesis 12:1 KJV

Okay, but why?

Like, if someone walked up to you and just said, "Follow me somewhere," wouldn't you ask why? In our relationship with God, we often feel like we are expected to just go along with whatever God says, often mindlessly. But that's not what God expects of us. I mean, not in the beginning of our relationship with Him, anyway.

For instance, with Abraham, God did not just nudge Abraham and expect him to follow blindly. No, our Father in Heaven sweetened the deal by offering him an incentive:

"And I will make of thee a great nation, and I will bless thee, and make thy name great; and thou shalt be a blessing: And I will bless them that bless thee, and curse him that curseth thee: and in thee shall all families of the earth be blessed."

— Genesis 12:2-3 KJV

Now we're talking!

If we go back to the previous chapter to read up about Abraham's history, we'll see that Abraham had come from a generation and a culture where things were not… ideal. A bunch of people had come together out of selfish ambition and planned to compete with God, sketching out a plan to build "a city and a tower, whose top may reach unto heaven." (Genesis 11:4 KJV) God saw their plans and scattered them, and Abraham was part of these scattered people.

I don't know, and this is just my personal speculation, but I feel like Abraham might have been excited to follow God to a better land than where he had come from. I imagine him being like the thousands of people all over the world, migrating to different countries in search of a better life. What's more, He had the solid backing of the Creator on his "*japa*" journey, as Nigerians call it; and a huge promise - he would be great! He would be blessed! His family would be blessed! If we think about it this way, it sounds like a pretty sweet deal.

It was only after Abraham received this blessing from God that he left his home land, to go on the adventure that has forever immortalised him as the Father of Faith.

When we consider our relationship with God, we often don't think of Him as the initiator. We often find ourselves wanting to offer Him our service, our actions, our devotion, as a way to get His attention. But even when it comes to the promise of Salvation, it is God who tugs at our hearts and draws us to Himself.

"No one is able to come to Me unless the Father Who sent Me attracts *and* draws him *and* gives him the desire to come to Me."

—John 6:44 AMPC

Look at the wording of this translation. It uses the words, "attract" and "desire" to describe the call of God to us. God doesn't demand, force, or command us to love Him; He wants us to have an emotional desire for Him. He attracts us, draws us to Himself.

Think about it. Let's say someone likes you. They've seen you around, and they think you're attractive, or smart, or something. Imagine that they just walk up to you and say, "I command you to love me!"

In today's day and age, you can even get the person arrested for harassment - depending on where you live, of course. However, there was a time - and there are some cultures - where it happens. But that's called slavery, forced marriage, sexual harassment, rape. That is not love.

Love can not be separated from free will; from consent. We must be free to choose: not coerced, manipulated or forced.

God knows this. He created the rules, principles and parameters of everything that governs or affects our existence. As such, when it comes to our relationship with Him, He loves us, first - He initiates, blesses, and convinces us to follow Him. And then, if we accept His affections toward us, we reciprocate that love.

"We love him, because he first loved us."

— 1 John 4:19 KJV

God in the Middle:

Just because He made the first move, He doesn't just sit back, like, "I called you first, now it's your turn to call Me back."

He actually continues to teach us how to love Him, helping us even when it's difficult for us to do so. We struggle to stay consistent, to stay committed, to spend time with Him, to respond when He nudges us… sometimes we don't even remember why He loves us, or that He loves us. And what does He do in response? He helps us.

He puts His love in our hearts:

"… the love of God is shed abroad in our hearts by the Holy Ghost which is given unto us."

— Romans 5:5 (KJV)

He helps us along the journey:

"But the Helper (Comforter, Advocate, Intercessor—Counselor, Strengthener, Standby), the Holy Spirit, whom the Father will send in My name [in My place, to represent Me and act on My behalf], He will teach you all things. And He will help you remember everything that I have told you."

—John 14:26 AMP

He even carries the burden of communication on our behalf:

"In the same way the Spirit [comes to us and] helps us in our weakness. We do not know what prayer to offer *or* how to offer it as we should, but the Spirit Himself [knows our need and at the right time] intercedes on our behalf with sighs *and* groanings too deep for words."

— Romans 8:26 AMP

God at the Finish Line:

All the way to the end, God is with us:

"being confident of this very thing, that He who has begun a good work in you will complete it..."

— Philippians 1:6 NKJV

"looking unto Jesus, the author and finisher of *our* faith ..."

— Hebrews 12:2 NKJV

"I am Alpha and Omega, the beginning and the ending, saith the Lord..."

— Revelation 1:8 KJV

We were never meant to feel alone on this journey of faith with God.

We were never supposed to shoulder the responsibility of the relationship between us and God, the Creator of the entire world. How could we possibly bear such a load? How could we ever compare? And what kind of God would leave us to try, without helping us along the way?

Would you ask your toddler to carry a heavy tray? Would you ask your teenage child to pay the bills? Would you ask the office assistant to find a way to generate enough income to pay the entire staff's salaries, at the end of the month? Not unless you were there, beside them, training them, teaching them, holding their hands at every step of the process. If we, with our limited minds, know that it is unfair to put a heavy burden on someone else without support, why do we think God would do that?

"If ye then, being evil, know how to give good gifts unto your children, how much more shall your Father which is in heaven give good things to them that ask him?"

— Matthew 7:11 KJV

"He who did not withhold *or* spare [even] His own Son but gave Him up for us all, will He not also with Him freely *and* graciously give us all [other] things?"

— Romans 8:32 AMPC

I want you to think back to every time you have felt pressured, forced, coerced or manipulated into loving God. Think about how it made you feel trapped, stuck, confused, or fearful. I want you to know that that was never God's intention, and I'm so sorry you had to endure that.

I'd like you to take a moment to note how you're feeling in this moment. Are you sceptical? Hopeful? Relieved? Angry? Whatever it is, please take a minute to write it down. If you're listening to this or reading a digital book, feel free to open your notes app, scribble a few words or draw what you feel, if that feels more natural.

____

—

____

—

____

—

God: The Judge of Injustice

'Uhm, Omotayo. I hear you on the whole love thing, but let's not take God for granted. He is also a Mighty Judge, and His Justice is just as much a part of Him, as His Love. You can't just focus on one side of His Nature. That's what has caused all the problems in the Church. Plus, we can't just erase the whole of the Old Testament and act like none of it ever happened, just because Jesus came to die for our sins."

I hear you. God is a Judge. He will not be mocked, and He will always exact Justice. But God's Justice is a reflection of His Love. In Psalm 89:14, the bible says, "Righteousness and Justice are the foundation of Your throne." However, it doesn't stop there. In the rest of the verse, the psalmist goes on to add, "…steadfast love and faithfulness go before You." That psalm actually begins with the declaration of God's Love, "I will sing of the Lord's great love, forever," Psalm 89:1 NIV

How does that work? How can Judgment, Justice and Love work together? The answer is actually quite simple.

To Judge, means, "to determine the result of" something, or, "to form a critical opinion" of something or someone. In the case of the legal use of the word, it means, "to hear a case", in addition to the other definitions.

The word "Just" means, "Of moral excellence", "Free from favouritism, bias, deception or self-interest", "conforming with established standards or rules", "Fair to all parties as dictated by reason and conscience". And, in that same vein, Justice means, "The determination of rights and the assignment of rewards and punishments."

A Judge's goal is to enact Justice. So, putting both definitions together, a Judge listens to a case, forms a critical opinion based on the information given, and then determines the result in a way that is fair, unbiased, and in alignment with established standards and rules of moral excellence.

The idea is that there is a way things should be, and the Judge is responsible for making sure things remain that way. And if people create situations that go against that way, that becomes an injustice and it needs to be corrected.

So, what is the way things should be?

When we look at our human existence on earth, we can see all the areas where there is injustice: poverty, sickness, corruption, violence, wickedness and unfairness abound. That was not God's original design. By looking at what He created, we get a glimpse of what He sees as Justice - that is, the established standards and rules of moral excellence.

First, God created a garden in Eden and put the Man inside it, to live there, to tend it and to have dominion over everything in it, and to be fruitful and multiply in it.

Eden means, "place of pleasure", "a delightful region", "state of great delight, happiness or contentment," "paradise". So, immediately, we see that God's first intention was for us to live in a state of happiness, contentment and delight. These are all emotion-terms: words that describe how we feel.

Then, God filled this garden with every tree that's good for food, everything they needed to fill their physical hunger. He then gave them work and a purpose, to fill their intellectual hunger. He gave them each other, to fill their relational hunger, and gave them Himself to fill their spiritual hunger.

This is the established structure that God intended for the world He created. He made the rules. He gave the guidelines and instructions, and He gave us the instructions on how to live in it.

And He never changed His mind. From the Old Testament to the New Testament, the epistles and modern day, He has always wanted us to live in a state ot delight, happiness and contentment, filled with the joy that comes from being in His presence, because He loves us. Psalm 16:11 says, "Thou wilt shew me the path of life: in thy presence is fulness of joy; at thy right hand there are pleasures for evermore." (KJV)

Therefore, every single time God sees His precious human beings living outside of this, it is an injustice. It is a lie, corrupting and misrepresenting His love for us, and He will Judge it fiercely.

And so, our God is a consuming fire, releasing His burning raging fire over every lie of the enemy. He will cast out, uproot and destroy every lie that is exalted against the knowledge of His Love. He will exhaust His Holy anger on every evil that stands in the way of His people receiving His Love. His wrath is relcased to destroy every obstacle that the devil puts in the path of His children.

Do you see?

Does this make sense? Write down what you feel, if you still have questions. At the end of the book go back through the questions you have and see if you feel clearer:

____

4 CHAPTER NAME

4. God: The Judge of Sin

"Okay, but how about God's judgment against us? Against sin, unholiness and disobedience?"

God's judgment of sin, and the theme of holiness that runs through the bible, also comes from His nature of Love.

To discuss this, let's look at what sin is, where it comes from and how it operates in our lives, and in the world.

In what is commonly known as the "Original" sin, God gave the Man and Woman an instruction, told them the repercussions they would experience if they disregarded His guidelines, but they did the exact thing He had told them not to do.

"...of the tree of the knowledge of good and evil you shall not eat, for in the day that you eat of it you shall surely die."

— Genesis 2:17 KJV

But the bigger question that plagues most people, when wondering about this incident, is this: Why was the tree there in the first place? We read about all the steps God took to craft and design the earth. So, if it was so bad, why did He include the tree of the knowledge of Good and Evil in His design?

Let's do a little bible study to find out. But before we go on, I want to suggest that it is not "challenging God" to wonder about His ways. In fact, when it comes to sin and righteousness, the Bible encourages us to be interested. Moses asked God:

"Now therefore, if I have found favour in your sight, please show me now your ways, that I may know you in order to find favour in your sight."

— Exodus 33:13 ESV

And so did David, the man after God's own heart:

"Make me to know your ways, O LORD; teach me your paths. Lead me in your truth and teach me, for you are the God of my salvation…"

— Psalm 25:4-5 ESV

We, too, can come boldly to the throne of Grace and ask for help. This time, we're asking about the tree of the knowledge of Good and Evil.

Now, after the man and woman had obeyed the devil, the bible records God saying the following words:

"Then the LORD God said, 'Behold, the man has become like one of us in knowing good and evil. Now, lest he reach out his hand and take also of the tree of life and eat, and live forever—" therefore the LORD God sent him out from the garden of Eden to work the ground from which he was taken. He drove out the man, and at the east of the garden of Eden he placed the cherubim and a flaming sword that turned every way to guard the way to the tree of life."

— Genesis 3:22-24 ESV

Let's break this passage down into different points.

From the first line ("the man **has become like one of us** in knowing good and evil"), it appears that the ability to know good and evil is God-like. If it is a part of God's nature, then can it be inherently evil? I don't believe so — but let's continue.

From the second sentence ("lest he … take also of the tree of life…"), it appears that the tree of life was another aspect of the God-head. In fact, we are taught that the Tree of Life represents Jesus, who also dies on a tree so that we would be able to "eat of Him[5]" and receive eternal salvation.

Now, because the man and woman would no longer be allowed to have access to the Tree of Life, the Lord sent them out "to work the ground from which he was taken".

But let's not rush past this. You see, when God created man, He gave them dominion over the fish, birds and creatures, but God was the One who caused the trees and plants to grow, and He was the One who gave it to them for food:

"And God said to them, 'Be fruitful and multiply and fill the earth and subdue it, and have dominion over the fish of the sea and over the birds of the heavens and over every living thing that moves on the earth." And God said, 'Behold, I have given you every plant yielding seed that is on the face of all the earth, and every tree with seed in its fruit. You shall have them for food."

— Genesis 1:28-29 ESV

They had dominion over "every living thing that moves", but it was the Lord who planted the garden. He made the trees grow and fed them from the trees and plants. Their work and their food were separated:

"And the LORD God planted a garden eastward in Eden; and there he put the man whom he had formed. And out of the ground made the LORD God to grow every tree that is pleasant to the sight, and good

[5] Matthew 26:26, 1 Corinthians 11:24

for food; the tree of life also in the midst of the garden, and the tree of knowledge of good and evil."

— Genesis 2:8-9 KJV

The man gave names to every animal, but we do not see the man having any interaction with the trees and plants except to use them as food:

"out of the ground the LORD God formed every beast of the field, and every fowl of the air; and brought them unto Adam to see what he would call them: and whatsoever Adam called every living creature, that was the name thereof. And Adam gave names to all cattle, and to the fowl of the air, and to every beast of the field…"

— Genesis 2:19-20 KJV

So, by the time God was telling man "to work the ground from which he was taken", He was basically saying, "Now, you'll have to find food, yourself."

But what would suddenly qualify the man and the woman to work the ground for food, if they hadn't been qualified to do that, before? What did they now have that they didn't have when God was the one planting the trees?

I suspect it was the knowledge of Good and Evil that they had acquired.

Especially because, during the Creation process, every time God finished creating something, He judged it as "good". I can imagine that He might have tweaked and adjusted a few things here and there when it was "not quite right" and only stopped when it was Good. That comes from the God-like ability to judge what is good from what is evil.

The next part of the passage in Genesis 3:22-24, says, "He drove out the man and at the east of the garden of Eden he placed the cherubim and a flaming sword that turned every way to guard the way to the tree of life."

He sent the man out of the garden where God was his sole provider, and so man became reliant on his knowledge of good and evil. The reality of our existence is evident that we have not yet figured out how to determine good from evil. In one era of history, black people were considered "scientifically" less intelligent - "evil". Today, it is evident that there is no difference in the intellectual capability of any race over the other - "good". There was a time when the earth was considered flat, and people who tried to prove that it was spherical were persecuted as evil. And even with less fundamental things; in one era, women are judged by their appearance and men are judged by their earning power. In another era, women are allowed to determine their appearance, and men are looking for partners who can share the financial burden with them. Human beings are constantly fluctuating in their judgment of what is good and what is evil. Because, even though they had eaten of the fruit, they did not have the missing piece: access to the tree of Life:

"... He placed the cherubim and a flaming sword that turned every way to guard the way to the tree of life."

— Genesis 3:24 ESV

The words, "to guard" stood out to me, immediately. God was protecting the way to the tree of Life.

Since we have come to understand that the Tree of Life represents Jesus, and we also know that Jesus is the Way, the Truth and the Life, I believe that the actions of God in Genesis 3:24 had a purpose. Beyond just the idea that He was angry or that He was lashing out and punishing the Man and the Woman, He was guarding or protecting the way to Jesus.

But if it 's true that we were made in God 's image and likeness, why would that be a problem? Why would the Man and the Woman be penalised for partaking in His nature? I believe that, in choosing to do the opposite of what God had said they should do, they showed that they were not ready for the responsibility that came with access to

Jesus. However, Jesus eventually came and offered His Life to us, which suggests that it was just a matter of time before we would have also been given access to the tree of the Knowledge of Good and Evil.

I believe that the tree of the knowledge of good and evil was not "sinful", in and of itself. I believe that the Knowledge of Good and Evil is part of the nature of God as a judge. God is Life and gives Life, but He also knows and discerns between Good and Evil - judgment and justice. So, both of those trees - as well as many others! - were present in the garden.

However: Justice alone can not lead to life.

"...for the letter killeth, but the spirit giveth life."

— 2 Corinthians 3:6 KJV

And what did God say to them in the garden?

"The tree of life was in the midst of the garden, and the tree of the knowledge of good and evil. [...] but of the tree of the knowledge of good and evil you shall not eat, for in the day that you eat of it you shall surely die."

— Genesis 2:9,17 KJV

We see that the tree of the Knowledge of Good and Evil "killed" the man and woman - in that it separated them from the presence of God, exactly like God said. But Jesus came that we may have life, and life more abundantly.

The question about why the tree of the Knowledge of Good and Evil exists at all, is the same question about the purpose of the Law, which Paul painstakingly answered in the letter to the Romans:

"If it had not been for the Law, I would not have recognised sin [...] But sin, finding an opportunity through the commandment [to express itself] produced in me every kind of coveting *and* selfish desire. [...] Sin...beguiled *and* completely deceived me, and using it as a

weapon killed me [separating me from God]."
— Romans 7:7,-11 AMP

This confirms to us that:

1: The tree itself was not the sin. It represents judgment, justice, the letter of the law. That is an active and present part of the nature of God.

2: Sin is something that has a will and a plan to lead us into destruction and death. Comparing this to what happened in the garden of Eden, we can make the connection between sin and the serpent, the devil, who comes only to steal, kill and destroy. So sin is not the tree - or the law. Sin is the spirit of deceit: embodied by the devil, the serpent, the deceiver.

3: If there hadn 't been any instruction, there would not be any thing like, "breaking the law". You can 't "break" what doesn 't exist. Basically, once the devil heard what we were not allowed to do, he decided that he would make us do exactly that. His only goal is to deceive us into doing the opposite of what God wants.

4: The outcome of doing the opposite of what God wants, is that we would be separated from Him. (Death).

It 's like, if you 're in a romantic relationship with someone, and the person says, "I don 't like it when people shout at me in public." If you then choose to do exactly that, then you would have created a separation between you and that person.

Eventually, if this continues, that separation would result in the death of the relationship.

In summary:

Why did God plant the tree? Because there 's nothing wrong with the tree.

Why did He tell them not to eat out of it? Because He didn 't want them to eat out of it. Some teachers have suggested that they would have been able to eat from it later - after eating from the tree of

Life - and from what we have studied, that is certainly plausible.

Why did He send them out of the garden? To protect the way to the tree of Life.

Why the suffering and hardship of the "curse"? That's just the nature of life outside the presence of God. In the garden, God planted and gave us food. Outside the garden, we had to work and toil for our own food.

Following this, then, what is God's relationship with sin, now? As the Righteous Judge, how does He reconcile His nature of Love with judgment of sin?

From the bible study we have just concluded, we can see that sin is not the forbidden fruit or the law. Sin is the spirit of deceit: embodied by the devil, the serpent, the deceiver.

The bible teaches us how spirits work:

"For what man knoweth the things of a man, save the spirit of man which is in him? even so the things of God knoweth no man, but the Spirit of God. Now we have received, not the spirit of the world, but the spirit which is of God; that we might know the things that are freely given to us of God."

— 2 Corinthians 2:11-12 KJV

Basically, the spirit of an entity - either God or man - lives inside the entity. In the same way, the spirit of sin dwells inside the devil. The bible also teaches us that whoever we obey is our master:

"Do you not know that if you present yourselves to anyone as obedient slaves, you are slaves of the one whom you obey, either of sin, which leads to death, or of obedience, which leads to righteousness? But thanks be to God, that you who were once slaves of sin have become obedient from the heart to the standard of teaching to which you were committed, and, having been set free from sin, have become slaves of righteousness."

— Romans 6:16-18 ESV

In His judgment - that is, His assessment and determination of circumstances, in alignment with established standards and rules of moral excellence, - the bible tells us that the payment for sin is death:

"For the wages of sin is death; but the gift of God is eternal life through Jesus Christ our Lord."

— Romans 6:23 KJV

Nothing else can fulfil the wrath of God except the separation of us from His Presence. When we obey the suggestions of the devil, we are separated from Eden, and everything we do in sin will yield us "thorns and thistles" as we labour in our own strength and our own understanding. That is the judgment of God on sin: that we will struggle when we are not in His Presence.

However, the way to the Tree of Life has been opened up to us. We are filled with the Spirit of God (not the spirit of the deceiver), and as such, the Sword of the Spirit now gives us access to Him. So we can repent - which means, we can change our minds. That is to say, even if we agreed with the spirit of sin in one moment, we can change our minds and turn back around to agree with God, the word, revealed to us through the Bible as explained and inspired by His Spirit within us.

We definitely experience moments of separation from God in a sense, but what is clear in the bible is that God will never leave us nor forsake us. From the Beginning to the Old Testament and the New Testament, that is one promise that we have not been able to "sin" ourselves out of. Let's look at a few:

"And, behold, I am with thee, and will keep thee in all places whither thou goest, and will bring thee again into this land; for I will not leave thee, until I have done that which I have spoken to thee of."

— Genesis 28:15 KJV

"And the Lord, He *is* the One who goes before you. He will be with you, He will not leave you nor forsake you; do not fear nor be

dismayed."
— Deuteronomy 31:8 NKJV

"If I ascend up into heaven, thou art there: if I make my bed in hell, behold, thou art there."
— Psalm 139:8 KJV

"... and, lo, I am with you always, even unto the end of the world. Amen."
— Matthew 28:20 KJV

"For I am persuaded, that neither death, nor life, nor angels, nor principalities, nor powers, nor things present, nor things to come, Nor height, nor depth, nor any other creature, shall be able to separate us from the love of God, which is in Christ Jesus our Lord."
— Romans 8:38-39 KJV

"...for he hath said, I will never leave thee, nor forsake thee."
— Hebrews 13:5 KJV

These promises repeated to Abraham, Noah, Jacob, Joshua, David, all the way to Jesus, show us God's heart for us. It is not His desire to be apart from us.

So, if 1) the wages of sin is death, 2) sin causes to experience separation from God, and 3) nothing can separate us from His Love, what does this tell us? Do we experience God's judgment in our daily lives on earth? And, if we do, what does that judgment look like?

I think it points to the fact that there must be a difference between God's judgment of death and separation from His presence, and the separation that we experience because of our actions.

For one, as Christians, we know that we have been saved by our belief and trust in the death and resurrection of Jesus on the cross:

"who Himself bore our sins in His own body on the tree, that we, having died to sins, might live for righteousness—by whose stripes you were healed."

— 1 Peter 2:24 NKJV

The Amplified version puts it this way:

"He personally carried our sins in His body on the cross [willingly offering Himself on it, as on an altar of sacrifice], so that we might die to sin [becoming immune from the penalty and power of sin] and live for righteousness; for by His wounds you [who believe] have been healed."

— 1 Peter 2:24 AMP

Again, we see God the initiator, even on the matter of this "saving from sin" issue. God did not wait for us to judge whether it was good or evil to be separated from Him, before He proactively offered Himself up as a sacrifice - to pay the penalty of death, so that we would be alive again. That is, if death is separation from His presence, then to be "alive with Christ" means that we would once again be "joined" or returned to His presence.

"But God, who is rich in mercy, because of His great love with which He loved us, even when we were dead in trespasses, made us alive together with Christ (by grace you have been saved),"

— Ephesians 2:1-5 NKJV

But God did not only atone for the sin of Christians; He atoned for everyone's sin — everyone in the entire world:

"And He [that same Jesus] is the propitiation for our sins [the atoning sacrifice that holds back the wrath of God that would otherwise be directed at us because of our sinful nature—our worldliness, our lifestyle]; and not for ours alone, but also for [the sins of all believers throughout] the whole world."

— 1 John 2:2 AMP

He "holds back the wrath of God that would otherwise be directed at us because of our sinful nature" — and He does this for **the whole**

world.

So, how does God judge sin?

First, the bible is clear that God judges the spirit of sin, embodied by the devil, the beast and the false prophet:

"And the devil that deceived them was cast into the lake of fire and brimstone, where the beast and the false prophet are, and shall be tormented day and night for ever and ever."

— Revelation 20:10 KJV

Death and hell were also judged:

"And the sea gave up the dead which were in it; and death and hell delivered up the dead which were in them [...] And death and hell were cast into the lake of fire. This is the second death."

— Revelation 20:13,14

The dead were also judged:

"and the dead were judged out of those things which were written in the books, according to their works. [...] And whosoever was not found written in the book of life was cast into the lake of fire."

— Revelation 20:12, 15 KJV

Here's what we can take away:

1. While we are alive, on this side of Life, Jesus' death "holds back the wrath of God that would otherwise be directed at us because of our sinful nature."
2. The final judgment - or, the "second death" - happens at the end of the age, not now, while we are alive on earth. This is important to note, because we have often believed that the trials and tribulations we face on earth are signs of God's judgment on us for our wrongdoings, but that is not biblically true.
3. When it comes to suffering and pain, the bible actually tells us

the following:

Trials and tribulations are part of our experience in this world:

"These things I have spoken unto you, that in me ye might have peace. In the world ye shall have tribulation: but be of good cheer; I have overcome the world."

—John 16:13 KJV

As Christians, trials should lead us to experience joy, because we understand that the hard times we experience are one of the tools God uses to work out patience, perseverance and character in us:

"My brethren, count it all joy when you fall into various trials,
[3] knowing that the testing of your faith produces patience. But let patience have *its* perfect work, that you may be [b]perfect and complete, lacking nothing."

—James 1:2-4 NKJV

In fact, our ability to find joy in the trials we face in the world, results in faith that is "tested by fire", producing the salvation of our souls:

"In this you greatly rejoice, though now for a little while, if need be, you have been grieved by various trials, that the genuineness of your faith, *being* much more precious than gold that perishes, though it is tested by fire, may be found to praise, honor, and glory at the revelation of Jesus Christ, whom having not seen you love. Though now you do not see *Him,* yet believing, you rejoice with joy inexpressible and full of glory, receiving the end of your faith—the salvation of *your* souls."

— 1 Peter 1:6-9 NKJV

Therefore, **the difficult experiences we have on earth are not "God's judgment"**. We have been saved from that by Christ's death on the cross. The only judgment left to face is the one at the end of the age.

4. Before Christ's sacrifice on the cross, however, it does appear that God judged sin with fire and death.

The Old Testament is full of encounters where people and nations experienced the wrath of God through fire and war, leading to the physical death of many. However, the bible tells us that these people were temporarily kept in a spiritual "holding cell" until Jesus died on the cross. And after He died, He went down to preach to them, the same way He preached to us when He was on the earth; giving them the same opportunity to repent and believe, that we have:

"by whom also He went and preached to the spirits in prison, who formerly were disobedient, when once the Divine longsuffering waited in the days of Noah, while *the* ark was being prepared, in which a few, that is, eight souls, were saved through water."

— 1 Peter 3:19-20 NKJV

"For for this cause was the gospel preached also to them that are dead, that they might be judged according to men in the flesh, but live according to God in the spirit."

— 1 Peter 4:6 KJV

In conclusion, it is clear to me that, even in judgment of sin and wrongdoing, God's justice is rooted in His Love for us:

"God isn 't late with His promise as some measure lateness. He is restraining himself on account of you, holding back the End because He doesn 't want anyone lost. He 's giving everyone space and time to change."

— 2 Peter 3:9 MSG

5 CHAPTER NAME

5. So, what's the point?

I heard the most honest statement from a Christian, the other day. It went something like this:

"The structure of church makes it difficult for people to ask the real questions they have, and be honest about whether they believe or not. So, people keep quiet and pretend to agree, so that they wouldn't upset the status quo. And when it comes to things like sacrifice and obedience, the truth is that I'm not interested in that. It's clearly part of what is expected in the faith, so I read my bible and pray — to essentially avoid being the worst person — but I'm disconnected from the religion."

I felt that so deeply in my heart.

Because I grew up with a Muslim father and a Christian mother, I used to feel very confident in being able to say that, unlike many people, I actually chose my faith.

On one hand, there was my father: a rather firm, but very logical, easy-going Muslim, who had built a career first as a core engineer and then as an entrepreneur who carved a niche for himself as a project manager within the civil engineering and construction space. On the other hand, was my mother: a somewhat shy but fiercely opinionated Christian, who was fiery when frustrated but reserved in public. A princess, the daughter of a knighted Oba (knighted by Queen Elizabeth II, herself), and a multifaceted creative who loved sewing, baking, gardening, she did not have the patience for structured entrepreneurship, having tried her hands at multiple creative business ventures without much traction.

I was also much closer to my dad as a young child; friends of my parents often called me his "handbag", as I clung to him whenever we were out. In sharp, and often bitter contrast, my mum and I were not friends. I could be quite well-behaved in general, but I was very rude to my mother. Whenever her friends visited, they followed me with their eyes, watching to see me act out. I never quite did – not around them, anyway – but my attitude was never that far away. And so, even apart from the fact that my dad was the head of our household and should have been able to Put His Foot Down regarding his children's faith, that would have been yet another reason for me to default to Islam; if only to show favouritism. Add to the fact that we also had weekly Arabic lessons where we learnt how to read the Quran, starting from the alphabets, some conjugation, and the most common prayers, and those are even more reasons why I could very easily have chosen to become a Muslim. On her end, my mother was limited to smuggling Holy Communion back home from church, teaching us how to pray when we were sick by quoting Isaiah, and whispering hurried prayers before my dad came back from work.

The last interesting tidbit I'll share is that I have four other siblings: all boys – well, all men, at this point. And while I have always been Christian, they've swayed back and forth over the years, with one of my brothers currently a self-declared agnostic. I would have suggested our catholic primary school as the culprit for my choice, but we all went to the same primary school and we did not all follow the same faith path.

So what really swayed me? How did I choose to believe in Jesus? Honestly, I do not know. I just know that I have never not been aware of the fact that I believed that Jesus was watching over me. It made me scared, as a child. I would lay awake and imagine Jesus walking into my room to try to talk to me and it would freak me out so badly. But it also comforted me to some degree, when I would have nightmares. My parents weren 't the comforting kind – after a certain age, I couldn 't come to them with tales of my night terrors – but I couldn 't sleep in a room alone with the lights off until I was an adult.

Maybe that was it: maybe I trusted Jesus because He was the Only One who promised to protect me from scary things. My mum taught me to call His Name when I was scared and I never stopped doing that. One way or the other, I found myself reading devotionals by candle-light when the electricity was off (which was more often than not, growing up in Lagos.) I had a bible under my bed because that was a form of protection from evil and I tried as much as possible to pray every night, before bed. I mean, I was still scared, but I had something to hold on to while I shut my eyes to escape the monsters.

When I was in my fourth year at university, one of my friends had an experience with the Lord that led her to make changes in her life. One of them was in her friendship circle: specifically, cutting me off. I confronted her and she tried to explain that she had had this encounter with Jesus but I didn 't understand what that had to do with no longer being my friend. I remember convincing her to go out to a party with us one night, even though she had insisted that she wasn 't interested in that anymore. That night, the guy driving us was so drunk that he was passing out behind the wheel. On the middle of the third mainland bridge. At some point, there was a massive trailer ahead of us and he was heading straight for it. We literally had to reach over from the back to turn the wheel to keep us from colliding into it. As soon as we got off the bridge, we called friends to pick us up and slept over at theirs for the night.

I didn 't think about it then, but I 've since wondered if that was the real reason she distanced herself from me. Somehow, I was the one who could convince her to turn her back on her promises to God. I was the Lot she had to part with; the hinderance to her fully surrendering to God 's call. It had hurt me so badly then, but I get it, now.

That said, it still scared me when I felt Jesus tugging on my heart in my mid-twenties. I didn 't want to be "like her": I didn 't want to cut off my friends and leave them with the same wound she had left in my heart. I remembered how I had cried because I missed my friend, and the thought of me being the cause of that pain for someone else kept me from responding to God sooner.

So, when the "opportunity" of romantic heartbreak presented itself, God took full advantage of it and I found myself finally crumbling to my knees and asking for His divine intervention in my love life.

It 's been about twelve years since I stood in front of my mirror – as if I was trying to look into God 's eyes – weeping and begging Him to teach me how to have His desires so that I could choose a sensible human man who wouldn't reject me, so that I would never have to feel this crushing pain, ever again. And, in that time, I learnt that I could hear God speak to me – me?! Undeserving, constantly sinning, me! I learnt that I could speak in tongues(!) I went from wondering whether everyone was just faking it to deciding there was no point to it (since we were already having conversations, anyway), then mustering up the courage to come out in the middle of church to have prayer warriors pray for me to receive the gift, only to experience the shame of being one of the faulty Christians who didn 't have enough faith - or whatever else we needed - to be blessed with it. The day I eventually spoke in tongues, it was just an uneventful little moment at the end of a regular church service. Holy Spirit whispered to my heart, asked me to try again with the stirring of faith I was feeling at the time. My first tongues started as a quiet whisper and then a torrent of slightly louder sounds, and no one knew it was happening except me and Jesus. It was such a sweet moment.

Well, after scaling that major hurdle, I figured I had won. I mean, not only could I converse with the Creator of the entire Universe, I could also speak in His supernatural language and say stuff that no one could understand except Him. Spiritually, I was the winner. I could even sleep in the dark without fear and Jesus had started showing me things in my dreams. There was nothing in this world or the next that could stress me out.

Right?

Lol.

As I grew to the point where I was open to having these beautiful spiritual experiences with Jesus, facilitated by the Holy Spirit, I grew more confident. Looking back, I might even say I was arrogant – or, maybe, naïve is more accurate.

I was part of different fellowships and gatherings and we grew in the study of the Word, we grew in faith, several people became ordained ministers and pastors, preaching and teaching the Word and moving powerfully in the things of the Spirit.

What I didn 't expect, was to know so much and still remain so… stuck.

I have cried, wept, begged, prayed and not had my prayers answered. I have heard God speak with clarity through me for other people, and watched my own dreams seemingly wind up in a fruitless dead-end. I have wept over words of prophesy that once stirred up faith, hope and rejoicing, only to cause whispers of, "Did God really say," and "Don 't be like that girl." I have spoken boldly about promises that have publicly fallen to pieces, and I have watched myself become what I have cynically termed, a cautionary tale. You know, that sister who is "so sold out for God", but," How come she 's not really doing much with her life? How come she 's still single? How come she 's... poor?"

If you 've been a practicing believer in Jesus for any significant length of time, you 've probably felt some of this: the pain of disappointment, the shame of failing after proclaiming great faith, the fear that you have somehow disappointed God, and that 's why "this is your life", bitterness toward the Word; sometimes directly shutting down any well-meaning bible quotes – because you know them all. You 've said them, all. And they have all failed to get you through the lowest, most painful seasons.

You might have shut down your dreams, ignore the nudging 's and silence the still, small voice you once took pleasure in; choosing to fill the spaces in your heart and mind with busy work, mindless scrolling or random company. Anything to keep you from being in any sort of place where Jesus might feel welcome enough to speak. You 've heard enough, and it didn 't take away the pain.

Christians talk about reverencing God, but they're actually afraid of God. We're like people who have learned to walk on eggshells around that rich uncle who occasionally hands out cash gifts - but only when he's in a good mood - and if you upset him, he'll punish you for years to come. So we keep quiet and hope he finds us worthy of a miracle, choking down resentment with Christianese quotes.

"God is good. All the time."

But we don't feel good. And it feels pointless.

In my deepest moments of despair, disappointment and depression, I lashed out at God. I told Him I thought He was wicked, that He could have made things easier and He chose to make them hard. My mind panicked and sent bible verses into the mainframe of my central processing unit, but my feelings were done with that. It felt like lies. I was isolated in my faith, I had nothing to show for my ability to hear God, I was embarrassed to be around my friends because I just knew they all felt sorry for me, and I was so deeply resentful. If I had chosen to go "the world's way", things would have been so much easier. Yes, I would have been depressed and I would have compromised my values, but even with all my values, I was still depressed.

So what was the point?

If suffering is part of our human experiences, what is the purpose of believing? What is the advantage of the Christian's choice to live a "consecrated" life while we live life on this earth? Why should we respond to a God who demands devotion and sacrifice, but does not follow through on His end, and instead gaslights us every time we have questions about His instructions?

The only reason I am still an active, believing Christian, is because, when I threw tantrums at the Most High, accused Him of being like the deceiver, was irreverent and badly behaved, did things that the structures institution of the church would call heretic, He never left me.

I don't mean that intellectually; like how people pretend to still be connected because they did their morning devotion and typed "Amen" into the fellowship group chat. I mean, I actually continued to feel - in my heart, through my emotions - that this Person was still hanging around.

You know how, when you're relatively okay with God, but you do something silly - like sleep over in your boyfriend's house, even though you know that the guy is not serious, and "something" (aka Holy Spirit, plus your common sense) has been telling you you need to stay away from him, but you ignore it, and then find out he had been cheating on you all this time. You know how you feel after, like you've just made your friend sad, and now you have to come back and find a way to beg your way back into their good graces?

I used that analogy to explain that, there are times when we feel disconnected from God because we know that God was trying to protect us and we disregarded it. So, there is a premise for feeling remorse, feeling sad, and knowing that we need to actively reconnect.

Well, imagine my shock and surprise, when I yelled at God in my disappointment and I didn't even feel *that* distance. That's what I mean. I felt seen, loved, understood, accepted. It was as if God knew that I was hurting, and didn't hold it against me. It was as if God did not make my pain about Himself. It was as if God was patient and kind and gentle with me in my despair. It was as if God understood what it means to love someone through their pain, without rejecting them in their weakest moments. It was as if God actually knew that I just needed to vent, to be angry, to cry. Like, He was strong enough to endure the intensity of my pain without being offended. Imagine that.

Many years ago, one of my friends lost her baby and she was devastated. We didn't find out for months, because there was no one around her to share the news and she eventually called one of us lashed out at. For the next few months, every time I called to check in on her, she lashed out at me, too. She said the meanest, harshest things I had ever heard. I felt bad, but I knew that it was not about me. She was hurting, badly. I kept calling her, I even fought back sometimes, but I would send a message apologising, or give her some space, and call again. It was not about me.

Let me tell you, yes, I can be a good friend, but I can also be extremely avoidant, clique-ish, overly analytic and critical. I go from being practical and confident to being sensitive and panicky. I tend to use my faith as a shield to avoid making tough decisions, then run to the other extreme and throw myself into tough situations to prove my faith. My point is, I can be a mess. And yet, I could tell that my friend's pain was not about me.

Why do we think we are kinder than God?

"If a son shall ask bread of any of you that is a father, will he give him a stone? or if he ask a fish, will he for a fish give him a serpent? Or if he shall ask an egg, will he offer him a scorpion? If ye then, being evil, know how to give good gifts unto your children: how much more shall your heavenly Father give the Holy Spirit to them that ask him?"

— Luke 11:11-13 KJV

Here's why:

Firstly, the institution of Christianity in the west is historically documented to have blended the practices and attributes of Roman gods and goddesses into the practice of the faith. Things like Easter, which was a pagan celebration, were overlayed with Christian practices, because the leaders of the day recognised religion as a useful tool to unify the different cultures they were leading. It was a strategic, political move.

On the Continent of Africa, we also merged our view of our traditional gods with the view of the Christian God, resulting in an approach to a God who is unapproachable, who needs a middle-man, who requires sacrifices, and whose wrath is harsh and punishing. Our Obas and chiefs had both spiritual and political influence, so we came to see the Kingship of God in the same light as the kings that ruled our communities.

Additionally, most of the people who have become teachers of the gospel, today, grew up without experiencing genuine love in their upbringing and their personal relationships. Many of them never experienced a parent be patient with their failure, show genuine concern and be kind. The, "I brought you into this world, and I can take you out!" mentality that many parents raised their children with, has made us see God as a temperamental Father, and the track-record of the Old Testament doesn't do much to prove otherwise. I hope that the bible study we've done so far in this book has helped to correct that a bit, but the truth is that it is only when we understand what Love really looks like that we can reset our expectations of God in a way that reflects His actual heart toward us. The bible teaches that God describes Himself as a King, a Father, a Mother, a General, a Friend, and because of that, we have learnt to see Him through the lens of our earthly fathers and friends, who might have rejected us and been harsh toward us.

I believe that that was His Purpose; that He uses those relationships to show the breadth of His Love toward us, as well as His desire for intimacy with us. In fact, He also uses other things to describe Himself. He describes Himself as door, a gate, a fortress, a mountain, wind, fire, light, even shadows. Bread, water, wine, a dove, a lion, a lamb, an eagle. God also calls Himself the, "many-breasted One", also owning the attributes of Femininity, something that scares the church to press into. But God is neither of these things alone; they are all descriptions to help us understand the nature of the Divine:

"For since the creation of the world His invisible *attributes* are clearly seen, being understood by the things that are made, *even* His eternal power and Godhead,"

— Romans 1:20 NKJV

God is the Original. And when it comes to our invitation to see Him in light of our human relationships, the other "fathers" and "kings" are copies, at best; and counterfeits, at worst.

Our parents, "kings" and deities disregarded our feelings, giving us "tough love" and telling us to, "snap out of it" and "stop being emotional", and so we think God is the same. People argue that "parents shouldn't be friends" with their children, so we ignore the fact that God actually wants us to relate with Him as a Best Friend.

I grew up in a home where hugging was not a thing; no one knew or cared when I was sad, and whenever my family saw me crying, it made them so uncomfortable that they would say, "I can't believe you're crying. Omotayo doesn't cry!" so how was I supposed to relate to the idea of a God who actually promised to wipe my tears?

And, yet, that was what got me. I mean, I started off thinking He was into trade-by-barter, as I had been taught to believe: go to church and He'll reward you. Pray and fast and He'll give you the desires of your heart. But, eventually, it was His, "I will never leave you nor forsake you," that has kept me. I tested the, "If I make my bed in hell", bit, and found that He really was there with me, down in the ugly dumps of rebellion and self-pity.

And that is the point.

Yes, the bible talks about us living sacrificial lives of devotion, forsaking earthly things and "carrying our cross"; joining Him in the fellowship of His suffering and enduring persecution for righteousness' sake. But, as we saw with the stories of Abraham in the Old Testament, and the disciples in the New Testament, it is God always initiates this Love relationship, He helps us in our difficulty and struggles **every step of the way**, and He always offers us a reward to sweeten the deal as He draws us close. It is only to the extent to which we are able to receive His Love that He requires any sacrifice from us.

The same church that says, "Love is not enough", "God doesn't care about our emotions" and prioritises faith as a "currency"; as if God is selling His Presence to the most sacrificial person, forgets that Faith is described in terms of expectation and reward:

"But without faith it is impossible to please him: for he that cometh to God must believe that he is, and that he is a rewarder of them that diligently seek him."

— Hebrews 11:6 KJV

The Fathers of Faith in that chapter were all invited into their journeys by a God who promised two things: to never leave them or forsake them - regardless of their bad behaviour -, and to reward them with things that they would see and experience:

Before you call me out and point out that verse 39 clearly states that they, "received not the promise", the fact is that they received the earthly part of what God promised. Rehab's life was saved, and she became one of Jesus' great-grandmothers. David got the crown and became known forever as, "the man after God's heart." Even Moses received the first part of what He was promised: victory over Pharaoh, as he successfully led the Israelites out of captivity by God's help. Verse 7 talks about Noah, who was saved from the destruction of the world. Verse 8 talks about the inheritance God promised Abraham - he got to live in Canaan, and he got to have not just the promised child, but several others.

However, the promises of God also pointed to a more eternal, spiritual Promise: Christ the Messiah; our Saviour. That was the promise that they didn't get to see with their physical eyes, and that was the promise that God kept, "that they without us should not be made perfect." (Hebrews 11:40 KJV).

God never calls us to live a sacrificial life without first drawing us in with His Love, affection and attentions. That would be slavery, coercion, manipulation, rape, bondage. It would be evil.

He draws us in with Love, with His own sacrifice, with His own gifts. And it is only when we receive them that He asks for a loving response from us.

It is like, if someone likes you and wants to get into a romantic relationship with you. They don't just ask you to start making sacrifices on the first day; they'll first woo you, prove themselves to you through consistent attention and affection. And it is only if you say yes to their proposal, and agree to enter into a committed relationship with them that they now have the right to expect you to reciprocate their efforts.

It is not enough for us to believe that He exists (even the demons believe). In order for our faith to actually please God, we must first receive His love, and also expect a reward; a sweet and loving relationship with Someone who is fiercely protective, loving, kind, patient and more committed to your well-being than you even are. That is the reward that He has promised. And, until we can believe that He really does love us **that much**, He does not expect a single sacrifice from us.

That may scare some of us. The idea that this sometimes scary, unfair, erratic God, can actually be patient and kind and loving and caring, feels like we're taking Him for granted. So let's look at our relationship analogy, again. If you would not enter into a relationship with someone who is harsh and unkind to you - like, that's just common sense, right? It's not enough to know that the person likes you, because people can like you and still use you, manipulate you, dump you, disrespect you. They have to earn your trust over time before you'll agree to enter into that relationship.

So, why do we think we are more reasonable than God? Why do we think we are fairer than God? Why do we think we are more considerate that God?

I mean, I know why: it's because we have been taught that God is a tyrant who can just snap His fingers and strike us with thunder and fire unless we obey. But even when we look through all the instances of God's wrath in the Old Testament, we see that He always initiated with Love. In the book of Isaiah, God is literally like a hurt, angry lover who misses His bride. Okay there are some threats here and there but I personally choose to ascribe them to the fact that Isaiah could have been taking God's pain extra personal. You know, like when your friend tells you that her boyfriend cheated, and you go and warn him with much more anger and venom than what your friend would have done. (But that's just my personal opinion!)

When it comes to the heart of God for us, it is clear that He values intimacy over piety. I know, I said it with my entire chest, and I'm not scared that God will strike me down - because He won't.

Yes, He corrects us and instructs us and builds us up and moulds us into His image, but the same way it is not your place to tell a stranger that they need to lose weight (yeah, remember the last time that happened to you and let it pinch your soul), it is only someone who has become close to you who can subtly say, "Uhh, friend, should we walk instead of taking the bus, today?"

"…Mercy triumphs over judgment."
—James 2:13 NKJV

I started my relationship with God thinking that He needed me to prove myself to Him before He could show me love and kindness.

I thought that once could do miracles, I would be spiritually invited to ask for whatever I wanted, but it didn't work that way and my heart was still resentful. I could still hear from God and prophesy, but it made me more disappointed when God didn't give me my own wish list. I could preach a sermon and get revelations from the Spirit, but I was still bitter. I could fast and pray and still be cynical. But His love - the fact that He cares about my feelings - that is the only thing did not change, and it is the only thing that no one can take away.

"Though I speak with the tongues of men and of angels, but have not love, I have become sounding brass or a clanging cymbal. [2] And though I have *the gift of* prophecy, and understand all mysteries and all knowledge, and though I have all faith, so that I could remove mountains, but have not love, I am nothing. [3] And though I bestow all my goods to feed *the poor,* and though I give my body [a]to be burned, but have not love, it profits me nothing.

"Love never fails. But whether *there are* prophecies, they will fail; whether *there are* tongues, they will cease; whether *there is* knowledge, it will vanish away.

"And now abide faith, hope, love, these three; but the greatest of these *is* love."

— 1 Corinthians 13:1-3,8,13 NKJV

6 CHAPTER NAME

Chapter: I want to believe, but **Believing is hard.**

At this point, I hope I've sold you on this whole, "God loves you", thing — for real, this time, not layered with guilt and fear.

If I have been even a tiny little bit successful, you might be wondering how to get involved in the whole thing. Like, in a real way, not just ticking the boxes of attending church every Sunday, pretending to believe that it makes sense.

Because, for a lot of us, even if we can try to accept that God wants a truly personal and intimate relationship with us, there's still the question of how to go about it. The last time you tried, it ended in even deeper disappointment and the church people you had grown to trust just ended up being like all the others.

So, let's take it away from the masses and the congregation, and let's start with you. Just you, with your personal history, your daily life's experiences, thoughts, your expectations and your needs (because, let's not even act like we don't want God to give us things, and that we still don't know how to trust that He'll actually give us anything.)

The starting point of faith is belief. That is, we have to believe in the whole miraculously impossible and, quite frankly, foolish story of the book of bible stories. We have to believe that the seas actually parted - literally, not figuratively. We have to believe that Lazarus walked out of the grave. We even have to believe that there was a time when people lived to be, like, six hundred years old. That's... a lot to expect a reasonable person to believe.

The reason why I'm breaking this down like this is that believing is **hard**.

They say, "all you have to do is believe!" as if it is normal to believe that listening to voices in your head is not the definition of insanity. As if it is easy to believe that some guy who you've never met died for you, when your own parents punished you because you got a C in your exams, or because you forgot to bring the chicken out from the freezer. Plus, you know what you did last night. Or, okay, it was last month. (I'm not judging!)

Believing is extremely difficult. You have to be convinced before you can believe in something. Like, even before buying a new phone, or voting for a politician, or agreeing to date someone, or even going to that party with your friends. That's why there's an entire marketing and advertising industry, because convincing people requires effort, intentionality, consistency, and proof that the product, or person is trustworthy. Even getting people to sign up for your free course, to watch your (free) funny video or subscribe to your free youtube channel is a struggle.

Following the theme of this book, I hope you can guess what I'm about to say, next: God knows this. He knows we're not stupid. He knows that our experiences have given us cause to "cancel" all religious leaders. Because of this, He has a multi-pronged approach.

Yes, He relies heavily on Word of Mouth to spread the good news. This is where people have personal experiences of His goodness and share it with other people.

"God healed me of my sickness!"

"Remember how I used to be addicted? I woke up one day and the desire is gone!"

"I used to be so anxious, but now I feel peace."

Etc, etc. From the woman at the well, to the disciples, our personal stories can be extremely impactful.

"And they have conquered him by the blood of the Lamb and by the word of their testimony."

— Revelation 12:11 ESV

It helps when these people are close to us, because it is more likely that we would have witnessed their struggle in some way, and then we can assess for ourselves if we believe that the change is significant enough to perk our interest. Sometimes, though, we find that even if the person has been healed of whatever ailment, their character remains nasty, and so we're just like, "Nah, not convinced." But, sometimes, it sticks.

At this point, you might be feeling like you need a practical example of how that happens. Like, how does God reach out? What does it look like? How will I know when I 'm experiencing it?

In the earlier chapters of this book, I touched on the fact that I can't quite put a finger on the moment I, "gave my life to Christ", as we say. I don't really remember a moment when I chose to hold God's hand in response to His invitation; especially because, through my mother's teachings, reinforced by my Catholic primary school attendance, it was already such a part of my life. But I do remember some of the moments where God wooed me in such a personalised, "Omotayo would like this" kind of way, leading to the choice to follow intentionally, and dedicate myself to Him.

The first "invitation" I remember was around the year, 2012. I had just been heartbroken yet again, and I had a moment where I decided, you know what, they say that if God chooses your spouse for you, then it'll work out perfectly and you would not have to experience heartache. So I figured the way to get Him to bring my husband was to "be a good girl". This meant, going to church, praying and reading my bible.

The church I chose was close to my parents' house, where I lived, and the pastor announced what was called a "discipleship course". I figured, you know what, I'll do it. Maybe I'll meet my husband there.

In the first few days of going through the accompanying workbook, I came across a bible passage that said, "By this shall all men know that ye are My disciples, if ye have love to one another" (John 13:35 KJV).

That verse pissed me off. Pardon my use of profanity, but I wanted you to feel the spark of anger I felt at the idea that love, mere love, was the essential distinguishing factor that would let "all men" know that we are followers of Christ. That was just ridiculous. I remember immediately thinking about Ellen Degeneres and thinking, "Ellen shows love! But she's not Christian. There are many people who are kind and warm and helpful in the world who do not believe in Jesus; so how could this be true?" But there it was, in the bible. Jesus clearly said that Love was the evidence that we were followers of Him. And not just the fact that we would know this love in a private way, but that the love would be visible enough to everyone, to the point that others would see it and it would bear witness to Jesus.

I didn't want to believe it (I thought it was completely ridiculous) but I had committed to this church thing and, while I wasn't sure whether or not God really cared about things like feelings and emotions, I still believed that I needed to get on His good side in order to get the marriage I wanted, so I was willing to at least see it through.

I shared my scepticism with my discipleship group, but no one had any real answers. Looking back, I don't think they knew what to say, except to agree with the words written in the bible. I mean, who was going to question God's word?

Enter: Omotayo. That question bugged me and I didn't let it go. The only problem was, I didn't know how to "hear" God. I got the whole, "kneel down, close your eyes, tell God you're thankful for all the stuff He's already done, so that He'll be willing to give you more stuff, which you will then recite," thing that we call prayer. But what if I had a question? How would I get it up to Him? And how would He respond? How would I know what He says back?

I was part of a different Christian email thread community at the time (yes, that was actually a thing!) and they had also asked this question about hearing God speak. Someone had responded with an example from the Christian fathers of old, and apparently one of them had used the example of asking God what tie to wear to work in the morning. You know, as practice. That sounded even more ridiculous than "love is the evidence that you're Christian", but like I said, I was committed to seeing it through. And, to be honest, I was also intrigued.

Anyway, one day, I stood in front of my wardrobe and decided to try asking God to pick out my outfit for the day. I said something along the lines of, "I'm going to run my fingers slowly over each of the clothes, and if I feel my hands stop on any of them, I'll take that as a sign that You're choosing that one."

Since we were all being ridiculous, what could it hurt? I figured this wasn't any more unrealistic than any of the stories in the bible so whatever, if God wanted to answer me He would answer me, and if He didn't that was up to Him.

But just as added insurance, I added, "If the item I choose is not Your choice, I'll still end up thinking it's Your choice, so if You don't want me to lie against You, please make sure I actually choose the one You want."

As I started running my hands through my clothes, I felt equal parts really stupid - and also hopeful. Obviously this was dumb - like, what would make my hands pause on an item? How would I know I wasn't just slowing down, or getting tired, or what if I was the one who thought, "oh, let's go with that"? My mind raced with different scenarios but my heart had this silly little excitement that said, "I don't care. I'm doing this, anyway."

I can't explain it, but my hand paused on a top and an accompanying bottom that I would probably not have thought to put together, myself, but I put it on, anyway. And when I looked in the mirror, it was such a stylish vibe.

I couldn't help it, I giggled - but I was also nervous. Like, did that just happen? Did God really answer me and decide to pick out my outfit for the day?

I practiced it again and again for many days after that. I tested the difference between how my hand paused when I asked God, and how I chose outfits when I was deciding by myself. And it was clear to me, that God answered me in a way that only Omotayo would know, only Omotayo would receive, only Omotayo would acknowledge.

Imagine if I took this experience and came up with: Five Steps to Hear What God Wants You To Wear Today. It would be foolish and deceitful.

The stories in the bible are illustrations of how God met each individual in equally personal contexts, and they are not actually descriptions or formulas of how God speaks to us. Some of them are similar, of course; in the same way someone's "Help me choose my tie" inspired my own experiment. But I don't know how God answered them, whether they threw all their ties up in the air and said, "God, let the one that lands first be the one." Maybe they looked at all the ties for five seconds then closed their eyes and said, "Lord, whichever one I see first in my mind's eye will be the one You've chosen." Or maybe he said, whichever one I feel like wearing, let that be the evidence that that's the one You want me to wear.

God meets us in a way that only we know: inside the depths of our hearts.

Philosophies, theories, formulas are common to many. Every human being can add two sticks to two sticks and end up with four sticks. That is a logical fact that is common to all.

Popular is the opposite of personal.

We learn from commonly shared theories; we learn how other people do things, in science, maths, tech, and even in law, policy, guidelines exist to conform everyone to a set of teachings.

That has its place in the way we navigate life.

But emotions are the only thing about our experience on this earth that are not common to everyone. No two people share the same internal feelings.

As such, when it comes to having a personal relationship with God, His ways are tailored to us — and the core of that; the, "who can know a man except his heart" part of us, is where He wants to meet us.

And so, there's nothing "practical" about how God pursues us, especially for anyone looking for clearly defined steps and formulas. While God gives wisdom and teaches knowledge, He wants access to our hearts, the only place where He can cut through all the reasons we have built up to protect ourselves from different forms of religious manipulation. By targeting our emotions, He bypasses our arguments and uses the least rational part of us to reach us. Of course, we have the bible, we have the ability to think and analyse. But, when it comes down to it, what God wants is an intimate connection with Him. He wants us to know and believe that He really and truly **sees us** and knows us. He wants us to know that we don't have to "put our best foot forward" with Him; we can feel safe, knowing that we are accepted.

Yes, He wants us to do the right thing and have moral standards and values, and be upright citizens of the world. But He is Home: where you can take off your suit and tie, fling off your wig and collapse on your bed, pick your nose, scratch your bum and fart without saying, "excuse me". You don't have to use your Presentation Voice to talk to Him, or send an official email with a formal introduction, body and conclusion, to make a request.

In my experience of God, He loves "inside jokes". He loves bonding moments. He loves hearing my gist. He loves it! Whatever your love language is, He's right there, with you. Words of affirmation? "I will never leave you nor forsake you." "You are altogether beautiful, my love, there is no flaw in you." "I have loved you with an everlasting love."

Quality time? "Draw near to God and He will draw near to you."

Acts of Service? "It is God who works in you to will and to do according to His good pleasure." Like, He does things for us because of His pleasure.

Gift giving? "Gave His only begotten son." "Give you every tree for food." "Have dominion"

The only thing I personally believe He needs our help with is physical touch: "Together with all the brethre, experience the length and breadth…" "love one another". "Kiss one another with a holy kiss" But I have experienced warm hugs that felt physically real in my dreams, so He has His ways.

We have had the wrong view of what God expects from us. The core thing He wants is for us to be loved. That is, to be able to believe that He loves us, to be able to receive that love, and to be so confident in that love that we truly know and live our lives with the confidence that nothing can make Him cut us off.

In His role as a Father, God will never disown us. Even in our weakness, He wants to be our Strength. When we don't know what to do, He wants to teach us, to remind us, through His Holy Spirit. When we do know what to do but are struggling with doing it, He wants to help us. When we feel hurt, He wants to comfort us. As a Bridegroom, He wants to He wants to Love on us. He wants to spend time with us. He wants to shower us with every good gift. As a Big Brother, He wants to defend us. He wants to carry the weight of responsibility for us. He has pleased the Father on our behalf, so that we would be confident to approach the Father through Him. As King, He wants to empower us with the authority to lead. He wants us to learn from Him, what it looks like to be a considerate, just and merciful Leader. In the battle of light and darkness on earth, He wants to empower us to enact justice against evil; casting out darkness and bringing light and sharing the same hope we have to others.

Before He asks us to "do" anything, He wants us to receive and accept His love. It is only His love that can shoe us who we are in truth; a mirror that reflects Christ to us until we are conformed to the same image.

"But we all, with open face beholding as in a glass the glory of the Lord, are changed into the same image from glory to glory, even as by the Spirit of the Lord."

— 2 Corinthians 3:18 KJV

It is in and through His Love that we start to see ourselves correctly: as people who are worthy of love, of devotion, of kindness, and everything good. It is because of His love that we can talk to Him and be confident that He will hear us, listen, that He will care enough to answer us. And it is through this loving relationship with Him that we can be confident that He will give us the answers to the questions we have, the wisdom to solve any issue, and the access to all the things He has promised us. The most eternal of which, is Himself.

"…that ye, being rooted and grounded in love, may be able to comprehend with all saints what is the breadth, and length, and depth, and height; and to know the love of Christ, which passeth knowledge, that ye might be filled with all the fulness of God."

— Ephesians 3:17-19 KJV

Part 2: How God uses emotions to speak to us, etc

Introduction to part 2:

The first part of this book has focused on the true heart of God for us, illustrated the significance of His nature of Love, and set the premise for our ability to receive His Love into our hearts, which is the seat of emotion. The premise of this book is that God works through our emotions to lead us into His Wisdom, which is premised on our capacity to receive His Love.

When you know the Creator of the universe cares about your outfit, your moods, carries your matter on His Head, you walk with the confidence of royalty. No one has to convince you, cajole you or force you to ask your Bridegroom whatever you want. You don't even need to check what He would say or think all the time, because you know your Father so well.

The idea of miracles, of authority, of manifestations, deep secrets and mysteries, realms, dimensions of heavenly things are not intimidating; you live with the Guy Who created them all, so all you need to do is hang out with Him and you'll be able to ask Him about it.

Love will make a parent leave their entire fortune for a child so that they would not have to suffer or sweat to live comfortably. Love will make a lover jump in front of a bullet for the person they love, even if that person upset them earlier in the same day. Love will make a King reveal the deepest secrets of His kingdom to His bride, so that she would be able to ask for things that no one else dares.

And love is felt in the heart, first: experienced through emotions.

It is only after we have been able to receive God's Love, that He can in turn have expectations from us.

And, oh, He definitely has expectations. We expect more from our spouses than from any other human being on earth. We expect more from our parents than any other human being on earth. We expect more from our close friends than the rest of our acquaintances. We also love them more than anyone else. That's just the way of life. But it is the love relationship that comes first: the expectations of reciprocity; the, "I expected you to be there for me" — all of that comes *after* we have experienced their love.

If you are reading this, and you have not yet decided to "marry" this Jesus who calls Himself your Bridegroom, I want to let you know categorically, that He does not need your church attendance, service or piety. You are only punishing yourself by forcing yourself to serve someone who you still think does not care about you. You might be in this situation because you did not even know that God's love was a thing, and so I hope I have been able to convince you that He does.

Now, if you are reading this, and you have experienced His Love, but you have also experienced deep disappointment with Him, I want to invite you to sit with your Father, Helper, Bridegroom, Big Brother, and let Him know you are not happy. Just be honest with Him about how you feel, and let Him respond in love to you.

You will know that you have entered into a true relationship based on Love, when no one can make you feel guilty for not praying enough, or reading your bible enough. Imagine your boss at work coming to tell you that your Father is disappointed in you? Or your teacher at school coming to tell you that your husband wants you to spend more time with him? Imagine the police officer telling you that you need to buy a gift for your best friend, or the traffic warden telling you that they your mother is angry with you?

All these people hold offices of authority, but their jurisdiction is clearly outlined: your boss is responsible for ensuring that you perform your previously outlined tasks, in service of the organisation you **both** work for.

Your teacher is responsible for instructing you on the established principles, theories and ideologies written in the course curriculum that has been previously vetted by the school administration, and not by the teacher's personal experience or opinion.

The police officer is trained to enforce the law, as it governs the public, and has no say on the relationship dynamics within your friendship group.

The traffic warden's focus is on the road, the cars and the smooth flow of traffic. As long as you did not have the argument while you were driving, and end up having an accident as a result, they have no business with your family.

In the same way, Apostles, Prophets, Evangelists, Pastors and Teachers of the gospel, have predetermined duties and responsibilities that guide their public office. They are appointed by God to serve the body of the church — that is, a collective group of people. And this specific group of people is also specified to these appointees by God. The same way there are many senators, but they represent the interests of different states or local governments. And the same way one might be reassigned to a different role, God can move or reassign people to different responsibilities to the body of the church, as well.

So, for instance, someone might be called to speak to women on the topic of singleness and dating. Another might be called to speak to men on the true meaning of masculinity. One might be called to serve government leaders by bringing God's prophetic counsel for the nation to them, and another might be called to evangelise specifically to people in prisons.

Earlier, we went over the difference between collective wisdom - maths formulas, chemical compositions, the laws of physics, the documented rule of law… that sort of thing - and the individual nuances of the "hidden man of the heart": our personal feelings. Understanding that, the roles in the church are appointed to administer knowledge and wisdom from God in the context of general knowledge to the people. That is to say, a teacher has the responsibility of explaining what has been written in the bible to people who don't understand; but the teacher is not responsible for mediating your personal relationship with God. That is why we can believe that God would test Abraham by asking him to sacrifice his son, but we know that we cannot turn that into a doctrine. The teacher who is taught by the Spirit of God has the responsibility to explain the difference to their specific congregation, but they can not prescribe what each individual should feel in their intimate moments of fellowship with the Spirit of the Most High.

A prophet appointed to a specific group of people, would have insight into what God wants for the group. Sometimes, that "group" vision can include highlighting the gifting of specific members of that group. However, in the individual's private space with Jesus, they would be able to discuss whether or not that is accurate, or even explore how that fits within the totality of the individual's life. Like, if it is true that the Lord wants you to move to another country, for instance; how would that affect His plans for your family? How does that work together with the vision He gave you for your work? It is in that intimate place that we can discuss the finer details with God and get clarity on how God wants to work the different elements together, working all things together for good.

The things God expects us to do in response to the things He tells us are also personalised. So, it makes sense that He might require a teacher of the gospel to spend five hours reading the bible and five hours praying in the spirit, daily. He might require an evangelist to fast for forty days and nights, because otherwise they would be too distracted. God might require someone to get married early, because their path is intertwined with the family they will marry into. And He might want another to take a vow of celibacy for a season, because their journey would require them to have the flexibility of solitude to move about without notice.

It is not for us to determine what we need to do as a prerequisite to receiving God's wisdom for us, or entering into God's allotment of gifts and authority for us on earth. The person who prays for five hours daily because they want to be called into the office of a prophet may be frustrated by their lack of growth, if they were called to something else, and if God's requirement from them was different. For instance, if God wants them to devote time to charity, they would be more spiritually anointed if they spent the same five hours cooking so that they could donate it to a food bank. They would see and experience more miracles dishing food to the homeless than staying up all night reciting prayers.

I have found that, in the areas in which I am exceptionally gifted, I can do more in one day than other people can do in one month, and I am not exaggerating. I have found that God can give me the idea for a book and teach me how to write it in two weeks, or even two days. However, even though I have the aptitude for other things - like business structure and financial models and even technical drawing - it would take me two years to be able to do what someone who is gifted at it can do in two weeks.

In the same way, spiritually, I have found that I can ask God for the answer to anything. I mean, literally, all I need to do is be interested in knowing His perspective, and I can run to Him saying, "Daddy, daddy! What do You think about this?"

But when it comes to helping people have these deep physical encounters with God, like people falling under the anointing and such, I have not found that I can express the Spirit of God in that way.

I will share the example of an event at church where a bunch of us were asked to pray for people. We were all young people in our twenties and thirties, and this was the first time anyone had asked us to do something like this; but we had been praying for there to be signs and wonders at the event, and we were ready to be tapped in as vessels for God to work through. My close friends went through the lines, praying for people and having them literally fall while they were praying. There was healing and deliverance everywhere! On my end, I whispered into people's ears, leading them to ask God what they needed and to ask God how He wanted to show up for them, asking them to tell me what He said in return, then hugged them until they felt safe enough to cry or whatever else they needed. Needless to say, my line moved very slowly. It was impactful, but **it was not the same**.

I have a friend who gets pictures and analogies when she talks to

God. Another friend has experiences with God; almost like He shows up in his mind's eye and hangs out with him. God loves it when I write or speak; He talks to me so much when I'm talking — and that matches my personality, perfectly. I also think out loud, and I get ideas, revelation, understanding and insight in the middle of conversations with my friends. And when I'm alone, I talk out loud — to myself, and to Him. And I feel seen, accepted, and loved.

I feel all those things inside my heart, and experience Him through my feelings and my emotions.

That said, it is important to understand that God does call us to "go ye into the world". This means that our personal private relationship with God is the foundation, but He does expect us to build on that foundation. He helps us, working in and through us, of course; but He still relies on us to agree, to yield our free will to His plans and purposes for us, in order to build on earth as it is in Heaven.

Our relationship with Him is guaranteed to last forever because He said so, but the impact that the world will be able to see is dependent on us responding to His invitation to participate in establishing His Kingdom on earth.

And so, in this section, I will explore how we can intentionally reach into the emotions of our hearts in order to receive God's wisdom and guidance in "building", within the following real-life contexts that we all find ourselves in:

5. Self awareness and personal development (also managing pressure and stress)
6. Decision making
7. Healthy sexuality and managing temptation
8. Leadership and community building (politics as an example)
9. Problem solving, insight, wisdom
10. Strategy: career, business, purpose, finance
11. Ideation & witty inventions (Science and Artificial Intelligence)

12. Conflict resolution in relationships: Dating, Marriage, Parenting
13. Generational curses and spiritual warfare.
14. Healing and the miraculous.

We will look at Emotions in more depth, using analogies from the natural world as well as the bible to provide deeper insight into how the unseen "realm" of our heart has been designed to function, so that we can partner with our mind and our will to access the depth of our emotions, as led, guided and submitted to, the Spirit of Jesus.

Let's go!

7 CHAPTER NAME

1. Emotions: The Love-gauge

If it is true that we can study the created things in the natural world in order to understand the nature of God, as in Romans 1:20 (NKJV), "For since the creation of the world His invisible *attributes* are clearly seen, being understood by the things that are made, *even* His eternal power and Godhead…", then we can look at the Creation story in Genesis 1 vs 3, where we see that the first thing God spoke into the earth was Light. We can then compare it with John chapter 1, where John describes Jesus as that Light that was released to the earth, and we can see in Romans 8:39 that the Love of God toward us is located in Jesus.

Following from that, let's look at the example of physical light to see what it shows us about the nature of God's Love.

According to elementary physics, Light can be absorbed, transmitted, reflected, or refracted.

Absorption of Light: This is what happens when Light hits a surface and is absorbed by it. An example of this is when green leaves absorb sunlight, in the process of photosynthesis.

Reflection: this is when Light hits a surface and bounces back. This is how our eyes see objects.

Transmission: this is what happens when light passes through an object. One example of this is light passing through a regular clear window.

Refraction: this is what happens when Light passes through water or

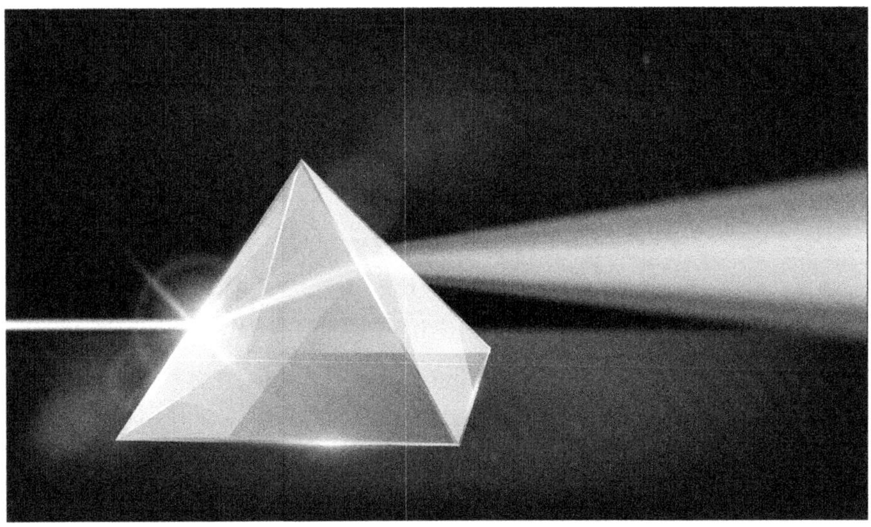

a prism and produces a rainbow, as seen in the image below:

"White light is composed of different components of a spectrum: red, orange, yellow, green, blue, indigo, and violet (ROYGBIV). When an object reflects all the components of light, it appears white. However, when an object absorbs all the components of light, it appears black." (https://abnercabuang.wordpress.com/2017/11/19/reflection-refraction-transmission-and-absorption-of-light/)

Even though all we see is white light, Light is actually made of seven different colours, represented by the rainbow. We see God showing us this after the flood in the bible, when He made a new covenant toward us and "refracted" His Light through the waters of the sky, giving us the Rainbow, in Genesis chapter 9. And if we replace the word, "Light" with "Love", following the premise we established earlier, then the rainbow teaches us that the Light of God's Love has different "spectrums" in the way we receive and experience it. He shines His Love on us, because that is His nature; however, we can receive and experience it in different ways.

Now, the part of our humanity that is responsible for receiving and experiencing God's Love is our hearts:

"the love of God is shed abroad in our hearts by the Holy Ghost which is given unto us."

— Romans 5:5 KJV

It is in our hearts that God shines the Light of His Love:

"For God, who commanded the light to shine out of darkness, hath shined in our hearts, to give the light of the knowledge of the glory of God in the face of Jesus Christ."

— 2 corinthians 4:6 KJV

Therefore, we can say that our hearts have the capacity to Absorb His Love, Transmit His Love, Reflect His Love, and Refract His Love.

This is where our emotions come in: **the very wide range of emotions we experience as human beings, are signals or indicators of the extent to which we are able to receive and respond to God's Love.** And, for all Christians who believe, we have the Spirit of God inside us, helping, teaching and guiding us to receive His Love into the hidden, hurting or hardened parts of our hearts where we struggle to believe that love really matters; or that God really cares.

This physics analogy is a helpful guide to help us understand the different functions our emotions, and how we can lean into them to understand ourselves, understand those around us, and understand God's heart for all of us, while we are present on earth.

Reflecting Emotions

Elementary physics teaches us that we need Light in order to see. It is because light reflects on surfaces, that our eyes are able to see different objects.

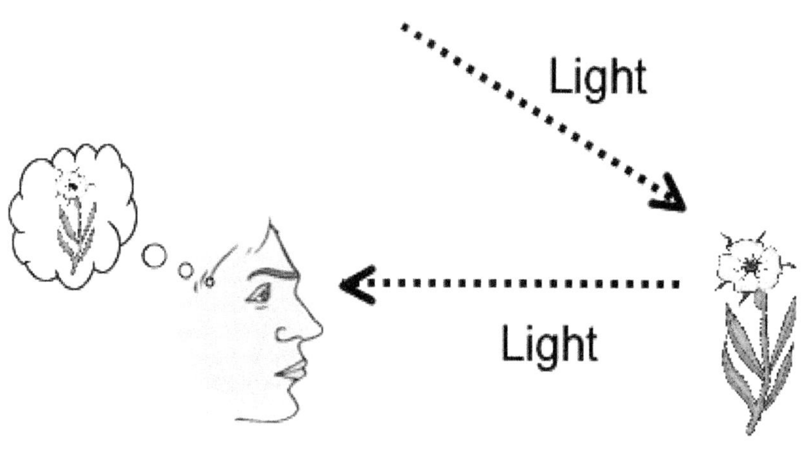

Using this analogy, we can say that our emotions are indicators of how well we are able to **see or recognise** the Light of God's Love.

Like most people, I grew up believing that God was far away in the sky and that it was our duty to pray in the morning and before bed in order to make Him happy with us. But I had a friend who would occasionally share things she would see in the bible, with me. One day, she shared Hebrews 11:40 (KJV):

"God having provided some better thing for us, that they without us should not be made perfect."

I remember being so shocked to see that. It felt like God was saying that He waited for us - people who hadn't even been born! - He held some of His gifts back from the Fathers of faith, so that the rest of us would also experience and be perfected by His Gifts. It's like, He knew some of His children had come into the fold, but He didn't want them to "finish everything" before the others came.

I was in university at the time and I was not familiar with the bible at all, but this was the first time I had thought about God as being such a kind and thoughtful God. I felt warmth inside me and realised that, maybe God was still scary and all - but He was also kind. It was not just a mental exercise of bible study, but the moment it connected with my emotions was when I knew it had become a real belief in my heart: I believed that God would not let His blessings "finish" before I got there. If He held something back from a whole Father Abraham, it could never be "too late" for me.

This experience helped me see the nature of God, clearer.

The bible tells us that it is when we see Him clearer that we can in turn, see ourselves better:

"But we all, with unveiled face, beholding as in a mirror the glory of the Lord, are being transformed into the same image from glory to glory, just as by the Spirit of the Lord."

— 2 Corinthians 3:18 NKJV

In contrast, I have already shared the story of how I felt when I read the verse about Love being the evidence that we are disciples. My immediate emotional reaction was anger and distrust. How could God say that?! My experience of Christianity definitely did not support that claim.

By recognising my emotions, I was able to see that I was quite far away from being able to believe what the bible was telling me. At another time in my life, I would have carried on with my skepticism, but because I was looking for God's favour and I had committed to following the process, I started asking questions to bridge the gap between where I was and what Gos's word said.

My emotions helped me recognise the distance I needed to cover in order to cross over from doubt to belief.

The bible is the clearest mirror we can look into to see who we are in Christ. It tells us that God loves us. It tells us that we are made in His image and His likeness. It tells us that we are "as Christ is", in this world. But even though we can read the words, recite them, declare them and pray with them, we don't often see ourselves the way God sees us. It can be hard to believe that we really look like Christ. We are so aware of our flaws that we think the "smudges" of sin are bad enough to erase our identity in Him.

So, even though His Light is shining on us, we often see a distorted reflection of ourselves. And because we don't see ourselves the way He sees us, we don't reflect the image and likeness that He intends for us.

"For if anyone is a hearer of the word and not a doer, he is like a man observing his natural face in a mirror; for he observes himself, goes away, and immediately forgets what kind of man he was. But he who looks into the perfect law of liberty and continues in it, and is not a forgetful hearer but a doer of the work, this one will be blessed in what he does."

— James 1:23-25 NKJV

Let 's paraphrase this in the context of God 's Love, which was sent through the Word - which is another name for Jesus:

"If anyone hears how much God loves us; - the lengths through which He Went to prove this love to us by dying for us - and is not able to receive it and respond to it, the person is like a man who looks in the mirror and forgets whether or not his face was clean or dirty; whether he was lightskinned or darkskinned. That 's because it is only in God 's Love that we can truly see ourselves how God sees us! In contrast, if anyone is able to recognise and receive the good news of God 's Love, and the freedom His Love has given us access to, that person will be able to live a life that shows evidence of the blessing of God in every aspect of their lives."

Our emotions help us honestly recognise and identify where we are, in context of seeing God's Love for us in truth. When we pay attention to how we are feeling, and when we don't try to push the feelings away or smother them with bible verses that we don't necessarily believe, our emotions become an honest reflection of the state of our hearts. And once we can see our own hearts honestly, we can surrender our doubts and unbelief to the Spirit of God inside us, and allow God to make His strength perfect in our weakness.

Examples of "reflecting" emotions are:

[make it a table: unclear reflections// clear reflections]

- Doubt and unbelief: not being sure is like looking at something and not quite being able to see it clearly. Either the image is unclear, or the image does not fit within your understanding, expectation or experience of what it should be. Either way, the image is clear - the light might be reflecting on it, but you are not able to recognise or accept what you're seeing. When we feel doubt and unbelief, Holy Spirit helps bring us clarity.

- Distrust and Scepticism: When our experiences don't match up with what we are being told to believe, it stirs up feelings of distrust within us. No one likes feeling like they are either being lied to, or taken advantage of. These emotions come up within us when we believe we are actually seeing quite clearly, and yet, someone else is trying to make us believe we're seeing incorrectly. When we feel distrust and scepticism, Holy Spirit helps bring validation or correction.

- Cynicism: When we have been hurt or disappointed in the past, we might respond to the idea of God's love with cynicism. We feel like it's possible that He loves people - you might have friends who have had significant testimonies and miracles - but it feels unfair because your pain has given you a different experience. When we feel cynicism, Holy Spirit helps bring healing, comfort and renewed hope.

Absorbing Emotions

When Light is absorbed, the object receives the energy and the qualities of the light into itself. For instance, when you leave something out in the sun for a while, it absorbs the heat of the sun, and anyone who touches that object for a while, would be able to experience a little bit of the sun's heat, through the object.

Another example is with plants and green leaves. Plants absorb the heat and properties of the sun and use it to grow and thrive. In turn, both human beings, insects and animals are able to enjoy these plants; using them as a source of food or shelter, and many other uses.

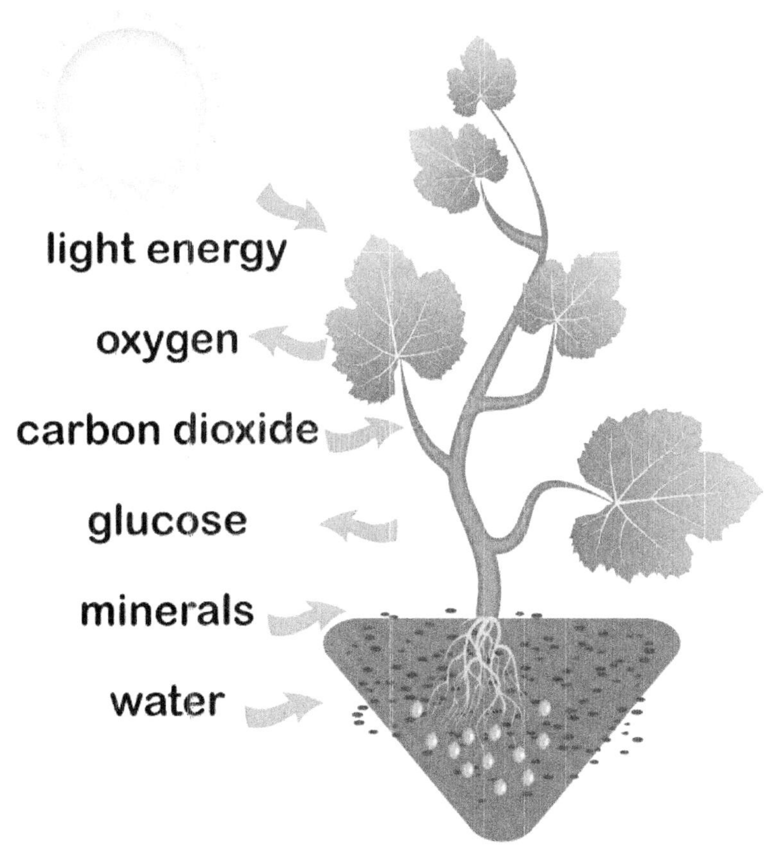

God wants us to be able to absorb His love, so that others would be able to experience the nature of His love when they interact with us. But the trials and imperfection of the world we live in can make that difficult.

Our emotions are indicators of how well we have been able to absorb God's love into our lives, and also how well we are able to share His Love with others around us.

"...that you, being rooted and grounded in love, may be able to comprehend with all the saints what *is* the width and length and depth and height—to know the love of Christ which passes knowledge; that you may be filled with all the fullness of God."

— Ephesians 3:17-19 NKJV

There was a season of my life when I really felt immersed in God's Love. I had been part of a close-knit fellowship, I had really good friends and we used to pray together often — I'm talking hours and hours praying in tongues, building up ourselves in our most holy faith, speaking and praying and prophesying over each other, encouraging each other, supporting each other, reading the bible and sharing revelation, almost every single day! And this went on for months at a stretch.

In this season, it was so easy for me to hear from God for others and for myself. My emotions became so clear, that I could tell when I was the one feeling something, and when the Holy Spirit was using that emotion to invite me to pray about something or someone else. I remember feeling troubled on a random afternoon and immediately praying for protection for a friend. A few hours later, the friend called me and had literally just avoided stepping on a nail on a construction site.

My heart was so full of love and peace and confidence in my relationship with God, that it was very easy to identify any emotion that contradicted that peace. As such, I could easily press in in prayer to find out what it was, and I would hear God's response and direction without confusion.

In contrast, I remember a different season when I went through a painful disappointment as a result of a failed romantic relationship. I felt rejected and I was angry with God, and I felt very distant from Him. In that season, there was a lot of confusion whenever I would muster the energy to pray. I had lost my sensitivity to His nudges and guidance. My emotions were all over the place and I could not discern my pain from God's voice. And even when I heard ministers or pastors, it would make me feel more confused: I couldn't tell whether I had lost my salvation and needed to recommit my life to Christ, or whether I was in a season of pruning and needed to surrender, or whether I was in a battle and needed to fight, or whether I was in the wilderness and needed to obey quickly:

"That we henceforth be no more children, tossed to and fro, and carried about by every wind of doctrine…"

— Ephesians 4:14 KJV

Yes, I still read the word. I still went to church. I was even still serving and volunteering. And I knew how to encourage myself by reciting bible promises to myself, but my emotions were the pointers that let me know that I did not believe it, not in that season.

The degree to which we have actually received His Love can be observed by paying attention to how we feel. When we are not full of God's Love, we are full of confusion, frustration, anxiety. When we are full of God's Love, we are at peace, we feel accepted, we are confident and full of joy.

Examples of "absorbing emotions" are:

[table: negative/painful | | positive/pleasurable]

- Rejection//Acceptance: We might feel rejected, isolated or misunderstood, those are indicators that we are not able to receive God's love in those areas of our lives where we've experienced those emotions. We might feel this way when we don 't agree or see things the same way other people do, or when we have experienced disconnection from people we expected to love and support us. It might be in a romantic context, like a breakup, or a "talking stage" that didn't work out; it might be with family, perhaps a parent who does not support your career choices. You might experience this with friends if you feel like you are not earning enough to keep up with the group dynamic, and it might even be with your church circle: you might feel like you no longer share the same values or goals. When we experience these feelings and surrender them to God, Holy Spirit affirms us, accepts us and comforts us, by reminding us of who God says we are, reminding us of our unique purpose and strengthening us in our time of weakness.

- Anxiety//Peace: Worry and anxiety are emotions that let us know that we have not been able to trust God in those areas of our lives. It might be because we have watched other people struggle on their journeys of "trusting God". Or because you don't think God is mindful of your personal struggles. You might be someone who thinks God has "bigger things" to worry about. When we are able to recognise these anxious feelings and surrender them to God, Holy Spirit helps us find rest and peace - even if the circumstances don't change, instantly.

- Rage//Joy: Emotions like rage, bitterness, anger and frustration can be very consuming. They are indicators that we feel like we are not able to control the circumstances that we are experiencing. As a result, we lash out and actually push love away, because it does not come in a form that we can receive. Or, because we feel like we have been disappointed by people who we expected more from. It can come across as righteous indignation, being critical and harsh, and feeling like you're doing the right thing - but it is an attempt to regain a sense of control. When we feel these emotions, Holy Spirit can turn it around and bring us to a place of peace, acceptance, and even joy — this is where we can find joy even in tribulation.

"Count it all joy when you face trials of various kinds"
— James 1:2-4

Transmitting emotions

Continuing with our physics analogy, light is "transmitted" when it simply passes through a surface without disruption. For example, light passing through a window is transmitted - it doesn't change form, and

it is not absorbed by the window:

In this image, the sunlight looks almost the same as if there was nothing between the viewer and the direct glare of the sun.

Our emotions can help us recognise how much of God's Love we are able to receive, and how much of it is just passing through us without leaving any impact - either on us, or on those around us.

Of course, we can have different degrees of "absorption" versus "transmission"; for most of us, there are some areas in our lives where we receive and radiate God's love. But there are others where we just can't relate. Using this analogy, the amount of colour in the glass determines how much of the light passes through. We will come to the significance of colour when we look at the last analogy of light.

"it has been given to you to know the mysteries of the kingdom of heaven, but to them it has not been given. For whoever has, to him more will be given, and he will have abundance; but whoever does not have, even what he has will be taken away from him. "

— Matthew 13:11-12 NKJV

With the context of our ability to see, receive and absorb God's Love, we can paraphrase this passage to read like this:

"The Spirit of God helps all Christians understand the mysteries of God's Love toward us. So, whoever responds and is able to receive and absorb God's love will receive even more love and more access to the things of God. But for anyone who doesn't have the capacity to absorb and receive God's love, His Light just pass through without any impact. And so the benefit of having Holy Spirit is pretty much pointless - he might as well not have it."

Okay, I took some poetic license in that re-version-ing, but the idea is that for those of us who have been given access to God's nature and love and His Spirit, we have a responsibility to ask Holy Spirit for help when we feel disconnected from His love. And, in response, Holy Spirit will help us receive and reconnect with God's love.

I have shared my single journey publicly, and one of the things I was most confident about was the fact that I had always had hope that I would be married and that was what kept me going. I loved the idea of love and, even though my relationships had not led to marriage, I had mostly dated good guys, men who had good core values, for the most part. I would always smile at wedding pictures and videos, loving the look of joy and bliss on the couples' faces as they looked at each other, and I would send up a prayer for their marriage to last, and for God to remember me. But a few years ago, I found myself growing cynical and completely disconnected from the love stories around me. I no longer believed that God had a plan for me to be married and, for a few months, I completely disconnected from the idea of marriage.

I didn't realise it was happening until one day, when I saw a pastor I admired announce her engagement and I found myself rolling my eyes and swiping away from the post. My heart noticed that this was not my normal emotional response, but I dismissed the alert. Weeks later, someone else who I admired - who I had even prayed for, in my quiet moments - announced her own engagement and I rolled my eyes, again! That's when I paused to assess what was going on.

It is because I knew my typical emotional response that I could identify when it had changed. And, because one of my core values is being able to celebrate with others, it became important to me to figure out what had gone wrong, and to try to return to hope.

It was not an easy process. It had been more comfortable to ignore and disconnect from the painful emotions of disappointment, rejection and pain, by becoming disinterested and apathetic about my romantic desires, but I did not like the new emotions I was expressing; that was not who I wanted to be.

It took a relatively long while, because I had to allow myself to feel my anger, to feel my pain, to feel the rejection. Avoiding those emotions did not take them away, it just changed aspects my personality.

For many of us, we have become so good at protecting ourselves from painful emotions that we have lost the ability to feel them. I remember speaking to someone close to me a while ago. I had been reminding them about a shared experience that had hurt me deeply; expecting that they would also share their pain with me. Instead, they said they don't feel anything. They acknowledged that it "could have been painful" for me, but they felt no connection to the experience and didn't feel anything about it. Of course, I can not impose my emotions on another person, but there is even some scientific evidence to show that we always experience emotion in some form or the other.

[insert science backing]

It didn't have to be the same emotion I had experienced, but they would have had an emotional response of some sort, to it.

I use this example to show that it is unusual to be so disconnected from our emotions that we feel, "nothing". That is one of the biggest indicators that we have either compartmentalised our emotions or we are avoiding them, altogether.

"For we have not a high priest that cannot be touched with the feeling of our infirmities; but one that hath been in all points tempted like as we are, yet **without sin.**"

— Hebrews 4:15 ASV

The ability to feel emotions is not only human, it is Christ-like. When we find ourselves unable to feel, it is an indicator that we need to ask Holy Spirit to help us regain sensitivity again.

" A new heart also will I give you, and a new spirit will I put within you: and I will take away the stony heart out of your flesh, and I will give you an heart of flesh. And I will put my spirit within you, and cause you to walk in my statutes, and ye shall keep my judgments, and do them."

— Ezekiel 36:26-27 KJV

Examples of "transmitting emotions" that let us know when we can't feel God's presence or love are:

- Apathy:
- Disconnection
- Disinterest
- Passiveness

Refracting emotions:

Sometimes, light goes through a surface and bends when it makes contact with it. That is what happens when objects look distorted in water, or in irregular shapes of glass. But when light itself passes

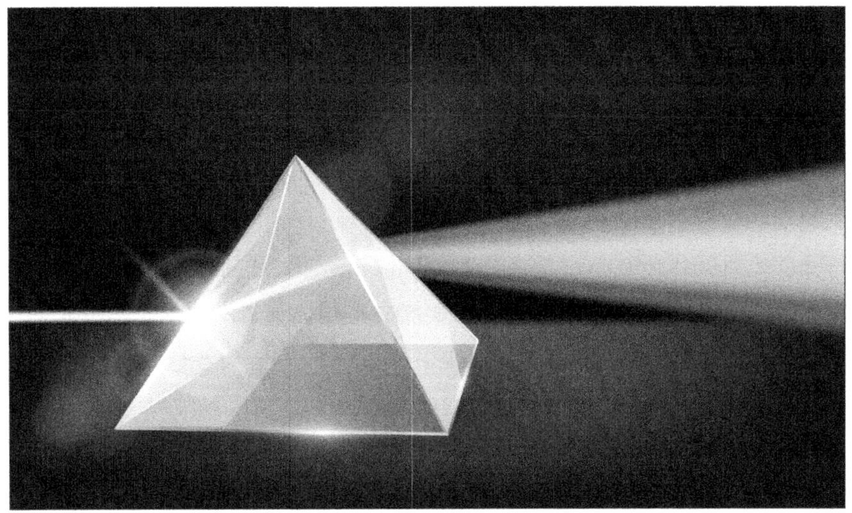

through water or a prism, it "bends" and produces a rainbow.

Following this analogy, when we receive God's Love into our hearts, and we respond to it by allowing Him to express His love **through** us to others around us, we are allowing God to work through us to "refract" His love through us, to the world.

Most of our emotions are indicators about our internal states, helping us identify how much of God's Love we have been able to receive, personally. However, the core difference between the other kinds of emotion and refracting emotions, is that these emotions are aimed at others. They are proactive and expressive, with the intentional goal of expressing God's love to other people in the specific, individual ways that God leads us to do so.

Of course, there's the general warmth that we should always radiate because we have absorbed His Love, but we will often be nudged by Holy Spirit to display a specific "colour" or nature or expression of His love, in a way that specifically matches the need of the individual you've been sent to attend to.

This often necessitates an **action that stirs up emotion**.

Like smiling at someone, or giving a hug, or being kind with no expectation. These are physical acts that stir up emotions in others. However, it is important to note that the acts alone are not the love. If you have ever received a cold hug, an empty smile, or had someone give you a gift, or give you money, without any joy, then you know the difference.

When people perform these acts just to tick boxes, they do not radiate love. They are simply regurgitating what they have seen or what they have been told to do, without being changed by God's love, themselves. Those actions do not convey God's love because emotions are necessary for connection. And we can recognise this lack of connection because our emotions are signals and indicators that let us know how much love we are able to receive, and how much love we have to give to others.

When emotion is not expressed, people don't feel seen, acknowledged or loved. They don't feel that personal physical touch of God's Love and, as we discussed under "reflection", it makes it difficult for us to see ourselves how God sees us.

Using the analogy of refraction, I like to think of the different colours as symbols of how "wide, long, deep…" God's Love is. And as Holy Spirit filled individuals, we get to allow ourselves to be led by God to show God's Love to others in the specific ways they need to feel Him. This is also an example of how intentional and mindful God is of us. He knows what each person needs, what they feel, and He knows how to meet us and touch our hearts in the specific ways we are yearning to feel His presence. By yielding to His leading within us, we can be intentional in engaging our emotions in ways that show God's Love to others.

In summary, refracting emotions are feelings we express toward others for the sake of helping them connect to the heart of God for them.

Even though we must be able to absorb God's love in order to express it in this way, we don't have to be perfect. Our human experience is multifaceted and complex, and there are different areas of our lives where we feel loved and others where we might be disconncted. To continue with our Light analogy, light sometimes can be reflecting, refracting, absorbing and transmitting at the same time. As long as we are yielded to the Spirit, we can be led by Him to express His love.

Examples of refracting emotions:

- The fruit of the Spirit
- Acceptance of others
- Generosity

Because this particular expression of Light is external-facing, we will spend more time looking through different aspects of life to make it practical.

SECTION 3:
How God uses our emotions to lead us to His wisdom in the different areas of our lives:

8 CHAPTER NAME

Using the analogy of the rainbow of His Love "refracting" through us, we can say that He uses a different colour to represent His heart for every different area of life. And while we know that God is far more multidimensional that just seven colours, we can use that as a starting point to see how God wants us to experience His Love in practical ways, and how our emotions are indicators to show us how we are currently experiencing His loving plan. By paying attention to how we feel, we can assess whether or not we are happy or content with where we are, and we can invite Holy Spirit to help us if we are not experiencing the fullness of His plans for us that we would prefer to be walking in.

I am using the following categories because they largely cover the primary areas of life that most of us engage in, in some way or the other. They are a helpful starting point to show how God's Love leads us into His plan for how we choose to show up in different areas, which are absolutely not limited to these seven.

1. Self-awareness:

   a. Sexuality

2. Spiritual awareness:
3. Relationships: Conflict resolution, forgiveness and boundaries
4. Education, Science and Technology
5. Creativity and the Arts
6. Business, career and finances
7. Government

Emotion versus Spirit

Before we explore these areas, it is important to make a distinction between the emotion of a thing and the spirit of a thing.

Emotions are physical experiences which can actually be measured in the limbic system of our brains. This includes the amygdala, the hypothalamus, cingulate cortex and the ventral tegmental area. Emotions are linked with our memories, our senses and our personalities.

Studying and understanding our emotions is as important as understanding our bodies. We all examine our bodies, even if it's only once a day, when we bathe. We know our physical anatomies enough to be able to recognise when something looks different: if there's a rash, a boil or bump somewhere, we are familiar enough with our bodies to immediately recognise those anomalies as things we need to investigate and, perhaps, treat.

On the other hand, spirits are supernatural living entities that have distinct characteristics that can be used to influence physical living beings. In order to influence us, spirits need to be hosted within the physical body that chooses, consciously, to receive those spirits. We see an example of this in the Bible where Jesus cast out evil spirits from a man, and into a herd of pigs[6]. These are different from other supernatural entities like angels and fallen angels, which also exist in the world but do not need host bodies in order to operate.

For instance, God is a Spirit who lives in us, in the form of the Holy Spirit. But while the bible documents instances where angels were sent on assignment, they visited and left. They do not live in us.

Now, the spirit of a thing expresses the nature of a thing, in the body it inhabits. For instance, the Holy Spirit expresses the nature of God in us. The nature of God is Love, and the Holy Spirit bears the fruit of Love, Joy, Peace, Patience, Kindness, Goodness, Gentleness and Self-control, in us. Because He lives in us, we also have access to

[6] Matthew 8:28-32

the eternal Wisdom of God, the Mind of Christ and the power and authority of the Spirit.

The devil also has evil spirits, which take on the nature of evil in various forms:

"… sexual immorality, impurity, sensuality, idolatry, sorcery, enmity, strife, jealousy, fits of anger, rivalries, dissensions, divisions, envy, drunkenness, orgies, and things like these. …"

— Galatians 5:19-21 ESV

While psychologists and deliverance ministers would be able to describe the difference between feelings and spirits in more depth, I shared this simple explanation to make it clear that there is a difference between the feeling of an emotion and the influence of a spirit through our emotions. It is because we understand what the emotion of love, joy and peace **feel like** — because we have a baseline for measuring the "temperature" of our emotions — that we can recognise when the Spirit is at work, expressing a particular nature of God inside us. In the same way, it is because we have a baseline understanding of what regular, cautious fear feels like, that we can identify the spirit of fear. It is because we know what regular anger, or disappointment, or sexual desire feels like, that we can recognise it when we feel an extremely controlling version of those feelings.

The more familiar we are with our regular human emotions - the ones that exist in our physical brains, and help us with core memories, relationships and our daily experience of life -, the more sensitive we will be to pick up on it when our feelings are expressing themselves in ways that seem intense, either positively or negatively.

If you're Christian, you're probably more afraid of the spirit of fear than any other emotion, because of the verse that tells us that God did not give us the spirit of fear.[7] That is certainly true; however God

[7] Timothy

definitely created us with the capacity to experience the emotion of fear. When we hear loud noises, when we're in strange places, standing on stage in front of many people, making speeches or presentations, starting businesses or taking risks, we experience the emotion of fear. That is healthy and normal.

Years ago, I had a friend who had an instruction from God to reach out to someone and share something quite vulnerable. This friend had been part of my close circle of friends who prayed together and had experienced the tangible presence of God for an extended season. We were always doing some sort of bible study or the other, getting revelation and encouraging each other in the Word, and I had watched her prophetic gifting strengthen and operate with razor sharp precision. So, when she told us what God had said, we bore witness to it in our spirits and we were sure it was the next step. All that was left was for her to take action.

But my friend froze. She was understandably scared, so we rallied round, reassuring her with prayer and encouragement. We had all had to do things that pushed us out of our comfort zone, so we understood. However, my friend didn't calm down. She continued to panic, and eventually decided that she was not going to respond to God's nudge. Over the next few weeks, her ability to spend time with God faded, because of the weight of avoiding this instruction. She became more panicky, more confused and more anxious.

It was a few months later when she finally decided to obey, and a few of us went with her, for moral - and spiritual - support. It was only when I saw her literally shaking, physically freaking out, throwing her phone away each time she picked it up, that I realised: oh, this is not just anxiety, this looks like a spirit of fear. On my end, I hadn't even thought the instruction had been that big of a deal. But even with multiple friends speaking in tongues, holding her hand and encouraging her, it took hours before she actually made the call.

She had endured months of anxiety, distance from her relationship with God, inability to hear or obey other instructions, because of the extreme fear of making a five minute phone call.

The emotion of fear, like most emotions, is fleeting. You hear a loud sound and jump, your body produces adrenaline, your heart races, and it eventually subsides. But the spirit of fear is crippling and debilitating: it starts to speak to you, to tell you things that are not true, to paint pictures of all kinds of things that can go wrong - even when they are completely unrealistic. You stop being able to tell the difference between reality and the weight of fear that has started to taint your perspective.

In trying to avoid our emotions, many of us become subject to the spirit of fear. We listen to the lies of the enemy, lying to us about all the things that can go wrong if we just get comfortable with being ourselves and feeling our feelings.

But for Christians who are filled by the Spirit of God, we have nothing to fear: especially not the spirit of fear.

Jesus gave us the power to cast out spirits:

"And these signs will accompany those who believe: in my name they will cast out demons; they will speak in new tongues; they will pick up serpents with their hands; and if they drink any deadly poison, it will not hurt them; they will lay their hands on the sick, and they will recover."

— Mark 16:17-18 ESV

And, funny thing, it's pretty easy to cast out spirits, actually. It's mostly just the spirit of fear that keeps us from boldly walking in the truth of what God says about us. You know, like how it took my friend months to make a five minute phone call. As Christians, all we need to do is literally ask Holy Spirit what to do, and then "do whatever He tells us", as Mary the mother of Jesus, said.

I have found that whenever I feel fear, all I need to do is open my mouth and say out loud, "Lord, I'm afraid. I don't want to be afraid."

By starting that conversation, I put my focus on the presence of God within me, and that is the first step in remembering that the same spirit that raised Christ from the dead actually hangs out inside me. From that point, as long as I stay in conversation with the Holy Spirit, I am reminded of His Love. And that is what casts out the spirit of fear:

"… perfect love casts out fear. For fear has to do with punishment, and whoever fears has not been perfected in love."

— 1 John 4:18 ESV

"Fear has to do with punishment." Let's take a moment to examine what that means. If fear has to do with punishment, and God has not given us the spirit of fear, then God does not want us to be concerned with punishment. And the confidence we are supposed to have, to keep us from fear, is this:

"And we have known and believed the love that God hath to us. God is love; and he that dwelleth in love dwelleth in God, and God in him. Herein is our love made perfect, **that we may have boldness in the day of judgment: because as he is, so are we in this world**."

— 1 John 4:16-17 KJV

There is power that comes with God's Love:

"For God hath not given us the spirit of fear; but of power, and of love, and of a sound mind."

— 2 Timothy 1:7 KJV

God's Love is the anchor that keeps us steady, whether we're experiencing physical emotions, or being influenced by the spirit of an emotion. We have nothing to fear.

Now that that's settled, let's go on to explore the different ways that God uses our emotions to lead us into His wisdom for our lives.

1. Self-awareness:

As human beings, we have the ability to feel and experience emotions with our hearts, the ability to think and reason with our minds, and the ability to use our will to make decisions. All of these aspects of our "inner man" work together, albeit in different ways.

When it comes to self-awareness, our emotions are the immediate first "sensors", picking up what we feel before we can think or process the situation. As a result of this, our emotions are responsible for what we call our, "intuition", "instinct" or "gut feeling".

It is important to highlight a few things:

- Our emotions are never incorrect or untrue. I know, we've been taught that they are unreliable, and before I explain why I can say this with full confidence, I want us to consider another analogy.

Picture a thermometer. You stick it under your tongue, or under your armpit like my childhood doctor used to do. After a few minutes, the thermometer shows you your temperature. Now, you might be too cold, or too warm, but **that is what you are**. The thermometer is an indicator of your current temperature at the moment of measurement.

It is after you acknowledge your existing temperature that you or your doctor can assess whether or not it is ideal, for the purpose of your health. The doctor can then move to the next step: taking the information presented and then recommending actions that you can take in order to return to an ideal temperature.

In the same way, our emotions are accurate indicators of how we feel. And it is based on the emotion we are currently experiencing, that we can assess what it means. Are we feeling loved? Unloved? Rejected? Frustrated? Unhappy?

Depending on what our emotions tell us, we can then decide process the information with our minds and decide what action we would like to take to either maintain the status quo, or move from one emotional state to the other.

- This leads us to the second thing we need to note: emotions can be influenced and changed; either consciously or unconsciously.

As human beings, we have the ability to "absorb" emotions; not only from God, but other people. When we are full of God's love - or, when we are confident, feeling positive and hopeful, at a state of rest, with no anxiety or frustration - it is less likely for us to pick up emotions unconsciously. Rather, it would be easier for us to recognise when we pick up emotions that are contrary to our state of peace.

I shared a personal example of this earlier: in the seasons when I was constantly filled with the Word, actively building myself in faith and surrounded by communities of praying friends, it was easy for me to pick up on other people's emotions, without internalising them. However, in seasons when I was not connecting with the Love of God, I couldn't tell the difference between my bad mood and the mood of the person next to me.

- Our ability to change our emotions consciously can also be a useful tool to help us navigate through difficult or unpleasant emotions, and to consciously bring ourselves into a place of peace.

For this, let's look at the analogy of a thermostat. In contrast to thermometers, which simply measure the existing temperature, thermostats are proactive: they have the capacity to change the temperature to the desired setting. In order to do this, however, we must be aware that the current temperature is not ideal, and we must have the desire to change it.

When it comes to our emotions, this means that we must be able to recognise the emotions we are feeling, in order to come to the realisation that we do not want to continue to feel the same way. It is at that point that our reasoning and thinking faculties come in, to begin to consider what we can do to change how we feel.

For Christians, we have the Spirit of God inside us, so we don't need to rely on our own mental capacity to make the change we desire. In fact, we are taught that we should *not* rely on our own understanding:

"Trust in the Lord with all thine heart; and lean not unto thine own understanding. In all thy ways acknowledge Him, and He shall direct thy paths. Be not wise in thine own eyes…"

— Proverbs 3:5-7 KJV

From the moment we recognise that we are experiencing unpleasant or uncomfortable emotions that we would prefer not to feel, we are not to use our own reasoning to make the change we want to see. For christians, what that means is that our immediate next response is to ask God for help. Literally just open our mouths - or whisper in our hearts -, "Holy Spirit, please help me. I don't want to feel this way."

A while ago, I got into a disagreement with a friend. We were both sure that we were right about our different perspectives, but it was also very tense emotionally and, by the time the conversation ended, I was still feeling deeply troubled.

What I wanted to do was call a friend to rant and vent my frustrations. That typically helps me feel a little bit better - even though I end up regretting it, because I care about all my friends and I never want one person to feel like I am exposing their weaknesses to other friends.

So I started talking to myself, out loud.

"Why am I so angry? No — I'm not angry, I'm hurt. Or, am I hurt *and* angry? I'm not sure. Okay, yes, I'm hurt and angry. But I'm also so troubled! And so restless! And so hurt! And so angry! I want to scream!"

On and on.

Normally, being able to articulate what I'm feeling helps reduce the intensity of my emotional experience, but it didn't work this time. That alerted me to the fact that I couldn't rely on my own understanding in this case, and I didn't know what else to do.

That's when I felt that gentle Holy Spirit nudge reminding me that I have a Helper and, if I'm honest, I wasn't in the mood to pray. I was so angry and upset that I didn't want to calm down to pray. If I'm even more honest, I felt like God would make it all my fault and take my friend's side.

But I felt the nudge again and I sighed in reluctant agreement. I still couldn't form the words to pray, so after an, "I don't know why I feel so bad, Lord!" I just decided to speak in tongues until the feeling subsided.

"Likewise the Spirit helps us in our weakness. For we do not know what to pray for as we ought, but the Spirit himself intercedes for us with groanings too deep for words. And he who searches the heart knows what is the mind of the Spirit, because the Spirit intercedes for the saints according to the will of God."

— Romans 8:26-27 ESV

The thing about praying in the Spirit is that our minds are still very much "in the natural", in the process. My emotions were still raging, and my mind was still struggling to make sense of my feelings.

But I felt Holy Spirit drawing my attention to what I was feeling: from hurt and anger, I was starting to feel guilt and shame. From guilt and shame, I moved to defensiveness. From defensiveness I moved to anger again, and then hurt and pain.

Holy Spirit then reminded me that shame and guilt are indicators that I was starting to think I was a bad person for not "getting over: the incident so quickly. You see, the bible teaches us that "there is now therefore no condemnation for they that are in Christ Jesus", so that internal condemnation was threatening to move me out of the confidence I have in the fact that God loves me, and that I was still "in Christ Jesus". That calmed me down a little. But why was I so hurt?

Holy Spirit reminded me of the value I have for this friend of mine, and reminded me that it is who we love that we feel more hurt by. And so, my feelings were only this intense because of how much I cared for my friend. That calmed me down a bit more.

But I was still hurt, and I realised I wanted a verdict: a judgment. I wanted to point fingers and draw lines: let's know who's wrong and who's right! And Holy Spirit nudged me again, reminding me that God loves both of us very much, and would never put my friend on blast to make me feel better. And before I could start feeling some type of way, God would never put me on blast to make my friend feel better, either.

Whew. Well. That finally calmed me down enough to be able to go to sleep.

I want to highlight the particularly uncomfortable emotions I felt in this process. The bible tells us that "the heart is desperately wicked, who can know it?" And there were moments when I definitely wanted to lash out and be unfair to my friend - even if it was only in my mind. But by inviting the Spirit of God into the process, I didn't have to be afraid of those feelings, because Holy Spirit helped me and guided me through it.

I received instruction from the beginning, as Holy Spirit nudged me to turn to God instead of to myself, or my friends. I received comfort for my pain, and not judgment for my weakness. I was reminded of the Word of God, and God's heart toward me, and I was not condemned for forgetting.

"The Helper, the Holy Spirit, whom the Father will send in My name, he will teach you all things and bring to your remembrance all that I have said to you."

—John 14: 26 ESV

For as long as we are led by the Spirit of God, our hearts are no longer evil and desperately wicked. The Lord renews our minds, giving us hearts of flesh: hearts that are sensitive to the correction and instruction of God.

Renewal is a process, and it means that we have to be willing to let submit ourselves as living sacrifices so that Holy Spirit would have free reign to point out the things in our hearts that are not in line with the nature of God. Thankfully, He is gentle even in the pruning, and the result is that we will be able to bear even more of the fruit of the Spirit.

"I beseech you therefore, brethren, by the mercies of God, that you present your bodies a living sacrifice, holy, acceptable to God, which is your reasonable service. And do not be conformed to this world, but be transformed by the renewing of your mind, that you may prove what is that good and acceptable and perfect will of God."

— Romans 12:1-2 NKJV

As christians, we are expected to present our entire bodies - spirit, soul and body - to God. Our souls are made up of our emotions as well as our minds and our will, so we must be willing to become comfortable with our emotions, even when they are uncomfortable, in order to be able to offer every part of us to Him.

The second part of that passage tells us why that is important: it will help us "learn to know God 's will for us, which is good and pleasing and perfect." (Romans 12:2 NLT)

9 CHAPTER NAME

<u>2. Sexuality:</u>

How can God use our emotions to lead us into His wisdom concerning our sexuality? Is this even possible? Well, the fact that you're reading this means I definitely believe so.

Our sexuality is part of our awareness of who we are and I was going to include it with the previous point, but I think it deserves to be addressed separately.

There are many religious and spiritual practices in our world that are very comfortable with different sexual practices, but in Christianity, it often seems as if sexual struggles are the dirtiest and the most evil of them all. As such, the subject is shrouded in shame and condemnation and, even though we experience everything from public sexual scandals to private personal doubts about what we can or can not do, the body of the church is particularly avoidant when it comes to this.

As such, the first thing I want to say is that feeling sexual desire is not a sin. The feelings can never be a sin. We know this because we all know that there is a difference between feeling hungry and eating food, or feeling angry and hitting someone. You might feel murderously angry at the person who hit your car in traffic and sped off, but you did not kill the person. The bible tells us that Jesus felt every single temptation that we felt, and yet, did not sin:

"For we do not have a High Priest who cannot sympathize with our weaknesses, but was in all points tempted as we are, yet without sin."

— Hebrews 4:15 NKJV

Did you see that? It says He was tempted **in all points.** It said Jesus was tempted **as we are**. That means, the same feelings you experience, He experienced it. And this is why:

"Because God's children are human beings—made of flesh and blood—the Son also became flesh and blood. For only as a human being could he die, and only by dying could he break the power of the devil, who had the power of death. Only in this way could he set free all who have lived their lives as slaves to the fear of dying."

— Hebrews 2:14-15 NLT

He intentionally made Himself partake of our "lowly" fleshly nature. The flesh that "profiteth nothing", Jesus took it on. He had to take on that nature in order to show us that it was possible to overcome it. And the "how" is the Spirit of God in us. In fact, the same Spirit that helped Him overcome, even when He felt tempted, is the same Spirit that will help us overcome when we experience the feelings of desire.

But, wait: sexual desire is not a sin. I really need this to be clear to all of us. Remember what we said earlier about the thermometer? That also applies, here. The presence of sexual desire is as normal as the presence of hunger. The same way we are responsible for making sure we eat healthy, we're also responsible for how we manage our sexual appetite. The same way we are responsible for ensuring that we don't use anger as an excuse for violence, we're also responsible for ensuring that we don't use our sexual desires as an excuse for abuse.

But ignoring sexual desire does not "cure" it — apart from the fact that there's nothing to "cure". One of the primary reasons why it can feel all-consuming is that we don't have practice with understanding our emotions, and we have a fear of sexual sin that stems from a misunderstanding of God's Love for us.

I don't have children, but I remember feeling like I was going to go to hell as a teenager, because I had all these feelings that I didn't know what to do with.

A few of my friends have children who are old enough to start asking questions about their bodies. I remember having a conversation with one of them, and she shared how intentional her and her husband were about making sure their kids could ask them about how they feel, their impulses, urges and curiosity about the opposite sex. It was awkward, but it was also important for them to make sure their kids knew that it was not wrong, and that they could ask them anything they were curious about. Listening to her, I felt this deep sense of gratitude on behalf of my younger self, who would have loved to have someone be willing to guide me through the reality of my feelings without the guilt and the shame.

Somehow, even though we can remember what we needed, and even though we can provide this comfort and understanding to our own children, we have somehow believed that God is a bad Father. That He does not care about us. We think He does not care, He's impatient and He's so irrational that, even though He is the One who wired us with sexual desire, He expects us to act like it doesn't exist. Again, we think we are more understanding, more realistic and more fair than He is.

If we did not think this, we would understand that He is patient, and kind, and gentle. That He wants to teach us everything about who we are, how we were made, and what we were made for. He wants to guide us through every part of our experience on earth, and there is nothing hidden from Him, anyway.

When we are honest with God about how we feel, when we invite Him into our most uncomfortable feelings, we give Him room to talk to us about them.

Whatever it is: feelings of attraction to the same gender, feelings of attraction to people outside the acceptable age bracket, young children who are curious about what's under aunty's skirt, tweens experimenting with what they saw on TV — it only grows from feeling to intention and to action because it wasn't first recognised and treated as real, human and something to understand, when it was just a feeling. When buried, ignored or avoided, these feelings grow into thoughts conceived in our minds, and then those thoughts become sinful actions.

The bible shows us how the progression happens:

"But each person is tempted when he is lured and enticed by his own desire. Then desire when it has conceived gives birth to sin, and sin when it is fully grown brings forth death."
— James 1:14-15 ESV

The desire is first. Again, at this point, it is not a sin. This is the point of intervention, where we acknowledge the desire and turn to our Teacher, Counsellor, Helper:

"If any of you lacks wisdom, let him ask God, who gives generously to all without reproach, and it will be given him."
— James 1:5 ESV

There is a lot more to explore within the topic of sexuality, but it is important to overcome the spirit of fear that shrouds this human feeling. It is this intense fear that leads most teachers and preachers of the gospel to avoid it, content with throwing bible verses at the problem and running to escape being tainted by it.

We all know that nature abhors a vacuum and, even worse, the bible tells us what happens when we leave spaces empty and "swept clean" without being filled with the presence of God: the devil takes up territory in every space that Christians leave empty.

I want to urge us to sit with our desires and feelings, inviting Holy Spirit into those spaces and not just assuming that we know what to expect God to say to us, in response. The crippling fear that makes us want to cringe, run and hide from this area is the spirit and not the physical feeling. It really is time for us to sit with our individual fears and struggles and invite the wisdom of God into the scary spaces in our hearts.

Spiritual awareness:

When I started writing this section, I suddenly started to feel anxious. I felt tired and sleepy, I felt stressed out, I felt like I wanted to sleep and, because I was getting really close to my deadline, I felt like I was failing. Then, I felt like I must be under attack to make me give up, but then that made me feel stressed because I didn't have the energy to start fighting a spiritual battle. Of course, the words I had just written came back to taunt me: specifically, where I'd shared that it's easy to cast out spirits once we allow ourselves to recognise them and lean on Holy Spirit for help. So then I turned to Holy Spirit but I was still silently freaking out. Normally, I would get up and start talking out loud to calm myself down, but I was at a library and I couldn't just start talking. All of this happened in, maybe five minutes and I wanted to shut down and just go home to hide under the covers for the rest of the day.

I felt a tiny nudge reminding me that, even though I couldn't talk out loud, I could open a separate document and just write out my thoughts, so I did. And once I had written the first sentence, Holy Spirit nudged me to use this experience to begin the chapter. So, I did.

Not up to five minutes into writing it, someone took my seat at the library - where I had been working for hours. As I got up to move, I realised that if it had happened when I was in the middle of the freak-out, I would have just gone home. Instead, I suddenly had something to focus on.

This is what it can look like to pay attention to our emotions. They are layered and complex; some are easier to recognise than others. But the thing about emotions is that they also move when we engage with them. To use yet another analogy, emotions are also like fire: they are ignited in response to what we see or experience, and there's smoke as the piece of wood or paper burns up. Our ability to recognise our emotions is like being able to see or smell the smoke, and follow the trail to find out what's at the root of it.

Ignoring emotions is like ignoring fires and hoping they'll burn out by themselves. Sometimes, they do, but they often create more damage in the process.

Spiritual sensitivity is absolutely impossible without our ability to pay attention to emotions. If we can not even discern what is truly going on within our own hearts, there is absolutely no way that we'll be able to discern what's happening beyond us.

When Jesus walked the earth, He spoke in parables, explaining that it was only the spiritually sensitive who would be able to understand that there was a deeper meaning beneath the stories:

"'For this people's heart has grown dull, and with their ears they can barely hear, and their eyes they have closed, lest they should see with their eyes and hear with their ears and understand with their heart and turn, and I would heal them.' But blessed are your eyes, for they see, and your ears, for they hear. For truly, I say to you, many prophets and righteous people longed to see what you see, and did not see it, and to hear what you hear, and did not hear it."

— Matthew 13:13-17 ESV

Hearts that are not sensitive or receptive, will not be able to see, hear and understand the things of the Spirit.

A lot of spiritual warfare happens in our minds, the Bible tells us. But our minds serve a slightly different purpose from our hearts: our hearts - the seat of our emotions - are accurate receptors and can discern different emotions, however complex, especially when surrendered to Holy Spirit. Our minds, on the other hand, are our reasoning faculties; where we process and make sense of information. Our minds process knowledge received through education, conversation, social cues, etc, as well as information picked up by our feelings. It is because we have both a mind and a heart that we can separate our actions from our feelings.

When it comes to spiritual warfare, the enemy works by introducing thoughts to our minds. If we accept these thoughts and receive them into our hearts, they will grow into weeds and thorns that compete with the seeds God has planted in us, already.

Let's look to the Garden of Eden to see how this works.

It was God who planted the trees in the garden, and that was how He designed it. The Man and Woman were only required to tend the garden: that is, take care of it, be fruitful and multiply what God had already initiated. The Man and the Woman were co-labourers with God, but God was the One who initiated everything that was planted and made.

This gives us a picture of how God wanted to operate with us: He always wants to be the initiator, and He only wants us to partner with Him to be fruitful and multiply. After all, we can not create our own seeds, we can only harvest the seeds that come from the trees and plants that God created.

The devil, on the other hand, has one goal: to steal, kill and destroy our relationship with and connection to the Father. Every form of spiritual warfare is aimed at this, in one way or the other. He does this much the same way as he did it in the garden, by inviting us to consider his thoughts and ideas.

When we look at the interaction between the Woman and the serpent, we have clues that point to what the Woman was feeling. She clearly felt hunger and desire: she, "saw that the tree was good for food, that it was pleasant to the eyes," (Genesis 3:6a NKJV), and those are natural physical feelings. There was nothing wrong with those emotions, because God, Himself had described the other fruits in the garden using those exact terms. In Genesis 2:9, the bible tells us this, "And out of the ground the LORD God made every tree grow that is pleasant to the sight and good for food." So, God was fine with them having those emotions.

As we discussed earlier, the knowledge of good and evil were not sinful, in and of themselves. God certainly knew good from evil, and throughout the creation process, He judged what He created as, "good", and He judged the Man's alone-ness, "not good". For as long as the Man and Woman lived in God's presence, they followed His lead and His judgment for them. They trusted Him to make the right decisions for them, and that was their only reality. When the serpent introduced the idea of them having their own ability to judge right from wrong, he did it by introducing a question, something to think about and consider. It didn't start from the heart, it started from the mind.

"Now the serpent was more cunning than any beast of the field which the LORD God had made. And he said to the woman, "Has God indeed said, 'You shall not eat of every tree of the garden'?"

— Genesis 3:1 NKJV

The serpent asked a question. Questions are processed in the mind, not in the heart. The heart already knows what it feels and what it wants. It does not engage in debates, it simply expresses its feelings.

Let's look at the thermometer analogy, again: a thermometer does not ask why the temperature is what it is. It simply reflects what the status is.

The heart can not change or influence itself: it is the mind that has the ability to influence it. Through the process of conscious questioning and reasoning, the mind can take in an idea and, in a manner of speaking, plant its own seeds into the soil of the heart, where it then grows into weeds and thorns.

In a conversation between the mind and the heart, the mind needs to pay attention to what the heart is sensing, and then use that information to determine its next steps. Ultimately, it is when the mind has made a decision - whether ot not it is in agreement with the heart - that the Will steps in to take action.

It is important to be able to make this distinction because it helps us understand exactly what goes on when we are tempted or attacked, spiritually. We can learn to discern; leaning into the characteristics of the heart to sense the "temperature" of the situation through our emotions, and using our minds to determine what course we want to take — all by the leading of the Holy Spirit within us.

And God will work in us to respond according to His perfect plan, which leads us to victory over every spiritual attack.

"But He answered and said, "Every plant which My heavenly Father has not planted will be uprooted. ""

— Matthew 15:13 NKJV

10 CHAPTER NAME

Honesty and Conflict Resolution in Relationships

Relationships are some of the most beautiful parts of our human experience and, as a result, they can also be some of the most stressful. We experience so many complex and layered emotions, those emotions collide with other people's emotions, we expect a lot more from each other, we misunderstand each other and it can be really difficult to give each other the benefit of doubt when we expect others to do the same for us.

When we take the time to understand our own emotions and we realise how complex they can be, it will help us understand that other people also experience complex emotions. Ideally, that should lead to empathy, but the bible tells us that our hearts are selfish and wicked when we are not filled with, and being led by the Holy Spirit. That's not to say that the presence of the Holy Spirit instantly takes away our selfish tendencies, but by consciously choosing to lay ourselves bare to the Lord, He can help us see through His own perspective, and bring us to understand that sometimes, the intensity of our emotions are a reflection of the value we place on the relationship.

The Old Testament of the bible is full of instances where God takes the form of a jealous Lover, calling out His Bride for running off to other gods. Those passages are often very strongly impassioned, and we can see the intensity of emotion God feels toward us. I know that anyone who has experienced infidelity from their spouse can relate to the intense feeling of anger and betrayal that follows adultery. When we look at those passages just thinking of God as a Spirit in the Sky that's detached from our real life emotions, it is easy to think He is erratic. But when we realise that God has emotions, that He shares those emotions and that He feels our emotions as well, we can reread those passages in the light of how you felt when you found out that your romantic partner had cheated on you. However, because God is ultimately God, because He is all-forgiving and because His ultimate goal is to bring us into reconciliation with Him, those passages in Isaiah and Ezekiel are often followed by pacifying statements, speaking of rewards and restoration once the erring bride comes back home to her Husband. For instance, in Ezekiel 16, God describes Jerusalem as a woman who He loved, clothed and protected, who ended up becoming a harlot. But from chapter 34, God is defending and fighting for His people, again. Remember, God created us in His image and likeness, so even though we are not Him, we look like Him — especially when we're being led by the Spirit.

When it comes to conflict resolution in relationships, I want to start by saying that feeling disappointed, hurt or angry is not a sin. Wanting to establish distance between you and some who has hurt you is not a sin, taking time to process your feelings is not a sin, and even deciding not to go forward with a relationship is not a sin. A lot of us hold on to relationships because of obligation or guilt, even though we have withdrawn from them, emotionally. The purpose of relationship is to enrich the individuals or glorify God, and if your relationship is not doing either of those things then it is no longer a relationship, it is now bondage and you are its slave.

Education, Science and Technology

Creativity and the Arts

Business, finance, career

Government

How God uses our foolish feelings to lead us into His Eternal Wisdom

My goal with this book was to show how Love - specifically, the Love of God toward us - is, not only the essence of the nature of God, but His motivation for creating us.

All human beings either receive and accept His Love, or reject it; and many of us are somewhere in-between.

Our emotions are the only accurate indicator of how much of that Love we believe, and how much of it we have received, at each point in time. Emotions do not lie because they are simply indicators; however, they can be complex and multi-layered, and we can experience seemingly contrasting emotions at the same time.

Our ability to understand our emotions works in partnership with our minds - our thoughts and our reasoning faculties - in order to influence our will, leading to our decisions and actions. However, Christians must always subject this process to the Spirit of God and not rely on our own understanding.

Because our emotions are always accurate, they are effective mirrors that help us see the truth of what is going on inside us, without the smokescreen of our thoughts, which are filled with facts, information and judgments of what "should" or should not be; what we are allowed to or not allowed to feel. Only our emotions can give an accurate diagnosis of what is in our hearts.

Because our emotions are not influenced by arguments and logic, they are our key to the subconscious realm of our brains; and by observing them we can easily access the deeply buried subconscious. By following the "smoke signal" of our emotions, we can easily sniff out the hidden "fires" in our souls.

Once this information is revealed, what we do with it is up to us. For the Christian, we are to subject it to the leading of the Spirit and not our own intellectual judgment. The Spirit of God will then lead us to the right decision for the moment.

We were not created to make judgments for ourselves that were separate from the judgment of God for our lives. Out minds were made to help us learn to trust God more and more, and not to create a separate system of judgment for ourselves. Our emotions keep us honest, and our minds help us invite God into our hearts, to teach us what to do to tend the soil that can be so susceptible to external suggestion and manipulation. Our minds were supposed to be able to guard and tend our hearts, much the same way the Man and the Woman were supposed to tend the garden: by following the instructions and the leading of God.

Our emotions belong entirely to us. God can not make us feel what we do not feel unless we invite Him in, or unless we reject Him. This is why believing and the faith journey is so individual, and that is why reciting empty bible verses, going to church and performing external rites do not convince God. Other people may see our externally pious actions, but He sees our hearts.

That is also where Free Will exists: our hearts feel what they feel, and it is up to us to determine how we will respond.

We can also make intellectual arguments even if we don't really believe them - our minds are versatile in that way. But we always know what we feel, even if we use words that say otherwise.

That's why, when it comes to the idea of sin, Jesus made it clear that it wasn't about a list of regulations. "Anyone who knows the right thing to do and does not do it, for him it is sin." That is the most personalised list of rules and regulations. Because it is only God and the individual who knows whether they knew what to do or not, whether they sensed it, whether they felt it, whether they believed it, whether they ignored the nudge.

ABOUT THE AUTHOR

Insert author bio text here. Insert author bio text here

Printed in Great Britain
by Amazon